THE

MORMON COUNTRY

AMS PRESS
NEW YORK

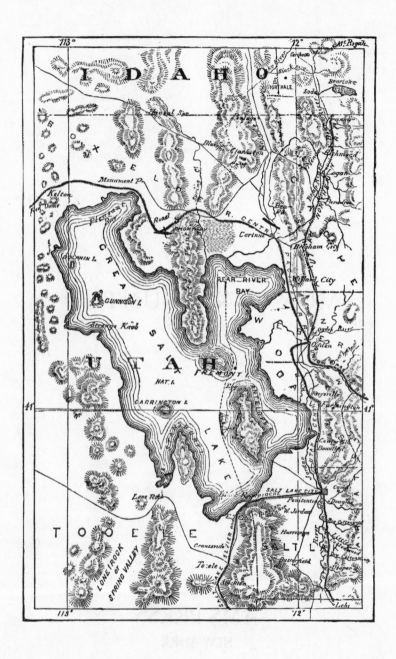

THE

MORMON COUNTRY.

A SUMMER

WITH THE

"LATTER-DAY SAINTS."

BY

JOHN CODMAN.

———

NEW YORK:

UNITED STATES PUBLISHING COMPANY,

13 UNIVERSITY PLACE.

1874.

Reprinted from the edition of 1874, New York
First AMS EDITION published 1971
Manufactured in the United States of America

International Standard Book Number: 0-404-08481-8

Library of Congress Catalog Number: 70-134392

AMS PRESS INC.
NEW YORK, N.Y. 10003

I T would be affectation studiously to avoid, or to apologize for the frequent use of a personal pronoun in a personal narrative. It is a necessity.

The manuscript was first offered to a prominent literary magazine. It was returned with the objection that it was too impartial. No higher praise is asked for the book.

When I parted from my old school-mate, HORACE F. CLARK, at Ogden, I said : " If I write a book I shall dedicate it to you."

It was his laudable ambition to control the great trans-continental railway lines of the United States. Had he lived, he would have succeeded ; and his honest and sagacious administration would have maintained the value of the roads, and developed the resources of the Great West to their most available capacity.

His death occasioned a loss to the material interests of his country, and is sincerely mourned by his numerous friends, one of whom

Inscribes this little Volume

As a Tribute

To his Memory.

THE MORMON COUNTRY.

CHAPTER I.

THE overland trip is becoming a fashionable relaxation. Improvements in railroad locomotion, by which nervous persons may spend days and nights in rapid motion and fancied security, decide the direction of their summer travel. Those who but for the wreck of the Atlantic, and the sinking of the Ville du Havre, might have "gone abroad," now discover that their own country has unsurpassed attractions. The Yosemite supplants Switzerland for romantic tourists, and Santa Barbara on the Pacific shore offers a cure for the clergyman's sore-throat equal to that of a voyage to Europe.

But in the haste with which our people generally congratulate themselves upon having "done" the overland journey, they are content to be whisked over the rails to their destination, making notes on the way of what they see from the windows of the cars, or at the restaurants where they are allowed twenty minutes for refreshments. A maudlin curiosity induces many travellers to time their arrival at Ogden on Saturday, so that they may branch off and spend Sunday at Salt Lake City, take a drive of an hour or two there, go to the Tabernacle meeting, see Brigham Young's house, if not Brigham himself, peep into some dwelling where a man is supposed to have more than one wife, and return in time to take the Sunday evening train for the West. They buy a big book written by Mr. Stenhouse, a small book by Mrs. Stenhouse, and the "Life of Bill Hickman, the Destroying Angel," and, having read up thoroughly, fill the cavities of their minds with details from these to supply what they did not learn from their extended visit of half a day. Thus they become perfectly informed as to the character and social status of the Mormon people.

I have varied somewhat from this usual routine, having passed three months chiefly among the Mormons, and have neglected reading the books referred to, with the exception of that of Mrs. Stenhouse, which came accidentally in my way. I stayed some weeks in Salt Lake City, and passed others in wagon and horseback journeys through the valleys and mountains, indebted to the hospitality of Mormon and Gentile alike, and am somewhat prepared to give an account of things that I saw, not of things as they ought or ought not to be.

Just before leaving I waited on President Young to pay a parting call. Expressing to him my obligations for the polite attentions of himself and of several members of his family, he said, "I am glad you have been civilly treated, but don't let that prejudice you in our favor. If you say anything about us, tell the truth." This is what I propose to do, in a running account of travel, with some comments on the social condition of the people and the agricultural and mineral resources of the country.

It will perhaps be remembered that in May last the late Hon. Horace F. Clark, President of the Union Pacific Railroad, visited Salt Lake City, in company with Speaker Blaine, and a party of other gentlemen and some ladies. The newspapers gave full accounts of their reception and of the impressions made by it. I was fortunate enough to arrive with them at Ogden, and there joining the party, participated in the attentions bestowed upon them.

At Ogden, which is also the junction of the Union and Central Pacific Railroads, the Utah Central, a profitable branch thirty-eight miles long, built and owned almost exclusively by Mormons, connects with Salt Lake City. It may here be remarked that the former policy of this people was seclusive, and consequently strongly opposed to all railroad enterprises. But when inevitable fate pushed the Union Pacific and Central Pacific lines across the continent directly through their territory, they wisely concluded to make the innovation profitable as it was unavoidable.

As will be seen in the course of this narrative, the rapid development of the mines of Utah has made not only this road highly remunerative, but is already extending it north and south, while other lines from the various mining cañons are being constructed to connect with it at Salt Lake City.

Our track lay for some distance along the borders of the lake itself, which extends to within fifteen miles of the town.

We arrived in a pouring rain, that continued for most of the time we were there. Had this been all that we could have seen of the city, most certainly our impressions of it would not have been very favorable.

On the next day Brigham Young, who was " unremitting in his attentions," gave us an excursion on the Utah Southern Railroad, intending to show us some of the mining districts in the cañons ; but it rained so hard that we were obliged to return, after going out thirty miles—Brigham jocosely remarking that "Utah was always under a cloud when viewed

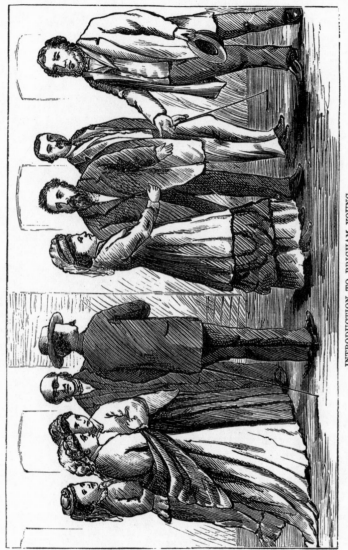

INTRODUCTION TO BRIGHAM YOUNG.

by congressional eyes, although everything was serene when the people were left to themselves."

We were accompanied by several of his small family, to whom, as well as to himself, the ladies of our party were introduced, their curiosity overcoming the indignation with which they regarded his over-doing the practice of matrimony. They admitted that he was certainly a very polite old gentleman, and they drew an argument in favor of their own sex from the consideration that a man who had been so very repeatedly and continually married, had arrived at the age of seventy-three in such a good state of preservation, without any appearance of having been henpecked. They reasoned very adroitly that if a man in Utah could stand against the aggregated temper of seventeen women, a man anywhere should not complain of the violence of one.

On the next day, Sunday, we attended church at the Tabernacle, an immense edifice capable of containing twelve thousand people, all of whom were present; for a large part of the population of the city and many from the adjoining country had turned out in honor of the occasion.

The order of exercises was much the same as in a Congregational Church, with the exception that there was an economy of time in the administration of the sacrament while the preaching was going on, and a change in the substitution of water for wine. Not did I notice in the hymns or prayers, or in the remarks of the first preacher, any peculiarity of doctrine which would have surprised me in one of our churches. This only appeared when Brigham followed the sermon with a few remarks of 'his own, evidently intended for Speaker Blaine, wherein he proved from the Bible conclusively to himself, if not to Mr. Blaine and the rest of us, that in their preaching the Mormons were in accordance with the teachings of Scripture, whereas he said all other denominations of Christians repudiated them.

Behind the pulpit were seated the choir, males on one side and females on the other, with a splendid organ at the end, said to be the largest in the country, with the exception of that in Boston. It is entirely of domestic workmanship, and in appearance and tone is a credit to the builder.

Brigham is an ultra-protectionist, and, as a worldly idol, would be worshipped in Pennsylvania. His great idea, before the advent of railroads, was to make Utah entirely independent of the outer world. He was on the high road to success, as proved by the specimens we saw in the museum. Utah can, if need be, provide every article of food and clothing that its people require, and in addition to these almost every luxury, including tobacco (the use of which is, however, discouraged), wines, silk, and possibly tea. Mills of every description abound in the territory, and almost every grain and fruit is indigenous to some part of the soil. All was to be of domestic production—food, clothing, and literature as well as religion, and so the organ was built here as an adjunct of the last.

On each side of the desk were seated the apostles and elders, men generally of advanced age. The congregation was neatly though not expensively dressed, and saving that the women, except in rare instances, were not disfigured by false hair and artificial humps, there was nothing particularly remarkable in the appearance of the crowd. Brigham bestowed his apostolic benediction alike on Mormon and Gentile,* and then we took the train for Ogden. From thence several of our party, including Mr. Blaine and Mr. Pullman, with their families, and the charmingly vivacious " Gail Hamilton," went on our way to California, it being the intention, afterwards realized by some of us, to return to Salt Lake.

Long will memory cherish the beauties of the great West beyond Utah ; the crossing of the Sierra Nevadas, so much more grand and picturesque than the Rocky Mountains ; the descent from their snowy summits to the luxuriant plains of the Pacific slope, waving

---

* In Utah every one not a Mormon is styled a " Gentile."

with grain and dotted with clumps of live-oak ; the inhaling of the balmy and delicious air where every breath was health ; the great city of San Francisco and its pleasant surroundings; and then, on our return, the visit to the Yosemite, that wonder of wonders, while the " Big Trees" we passed on our approach to it still loom up in the vista of pleasing remembrance, each tree a forest of itself.

Nor did we forget to linger a few days at Lake Tahoe, on the western side of the Sierras, six thousand five hundred feet above the level of the sea, thirty-five miles in length, fringed by mountains of everlasting snow, of clear, transparent depths, full of great salmon-trout that came so readily to our hooks. And then we returned to Salt Lake City, for we had promised Mr. John W. Young that we should be there on the last of June.

CHAPTER II.

FAR different was the appearance of the city from that presented to us in the rain-storms of May. Now the weather was settled and bright, the harvests were ripe for the sickle, the trees were loaded with fruit, and all things wore faces of smiles.

Imagine a city of twenty-five thousand inhabitants, each dwelling-house in a garden enclosure of one and a quarter acre, full of trees and vines ; all the streets wide, and intersecting each other as they run from north to south and east to west ; on both sides of every one of them a clear running stream of water supplied from the hills, so that every man may irrigate his land with the least possible trouble and expense. Thus is Salt Lake City and every town in the territory laid out. The soil, when not watered, is a barren, alkaline desert ; when it is watered it is a lovely garden.

Nature has been conquered by the hand of man, and accepts her defeat with smiles.

Nor is it only in the towns that the system of irrigation prevails. Thousands and tens of thousands of acres of farm-land are thus rescued from inactivity, and now produce fifty bushels of wheat to the acre where nothing but wild sage-brush would formerly grow. When the recent foundation of the city is considered, it will not seem surprising that many of the houses are still small and unpretentious, some of the old adobe shanties yet remaining. But these are rapidly giving place to large and expensive houses of brick and stone. There are several first-class hotels which would do credit to any eastern city. Among the public buildings most worthy of mention is the Tabernacle—chiefly remarkable for its size, for it has no beauty—the city hall, and the theatre, recently renovated and always well attended. The city is remarkably clean and healthy. This is owing not only to the salubrity of the air, but to the running waters in the streets. The domains of Brigham Young are secluded behind high walls. Although he is the wealthiest man in the place, his house is simple in its architecture and far less costly than many others belonging to rich Mormons and Gentiles.

We happened to be in town on the Fourth of July. The day was celebrated in the usual style by orations

and fire-crackers.   There were also excursions to the
cañons, and on the only steamboat on Salt Lake.
But the 24th of July is the special Mormon holiday, that being the anniversary of the arrival of
the Saints upon these plains.   On the 24th I was
away in the mountains, and do not know how much
general patriotism was mingled with territorial rights;
but on the day of national independence, whatever
may have been the former antagonism of the people
to the United States authorities, there was nothing
of the kind apparent now.   The star-spangled banner
was waved as exultingly by them as by any people
of this broad land, and they were as loud as any of
us in their protestations of allegiance.

On the 5th of July I left the city with Mr. John
W. Young, at his invitation, for a tour to the North.
Again passing over the Utah Central Railroad to
Ogden, we were taken on the Central Pacific to the
westward for twenty-four miles to Corinne, where
we took the narrow-gauge railroad, then completed
for forty miles north to Logan.

This road is now the pet scheme of my friend, John
W. Young, but it owes its inception and construction
chiefly to the enterprise of a single eastern capitalist,
Joseph Richardson, Esq., of New York.   That gentleman surveyed the whole of its route by patient foot-
journeys, and became so well satisfied of its feasibility

that he invested a fortune in its stock, and is now fur-
nishing its iron, engines, cars, and equipments. Besides the branch on which we started from Corinne, its
main trunk is already finished. This diverges from
Ogden, thus connecting with the Utah Central by
crossing the junction of the Union Pacific and Central
Pacific Railroads. Its first support in the line of trade
comes from the iron mines at Willard's, fifteen miles
north of Ogden. Thirty tons of this ore have been
hauled daily by tedious wagon-trains, destined for
the smelting-works at Sandy, and now the railroad
facilities will largely increase the production, especially
as a Pittsburgh company is putting up iron-works at
Ogden itself.

Seven miles north of Willard's the road reaches
Brigham City, one of the largest and most thriving
Mormon settlements, to which I shall have occasion
to refer again. At this place are the extensive co-
operative woollen factories and tanneries, giving em-
ployment to a large number of hands, and finding a
home-market in the territory as well as a large sale
for their products abroad.

The next place of interest is Hampton, twenty miles
still further north. Here are the stone-quarries, producing an excellent building-material, used by the
Mormons for the construction of many of their public and private edifices.

It may be mentioned that while our enterprising friend, Mr. Richardson, has such intimate business relations with this people, he is himself a devout Episcopalian, and that he has followed the suggestions of Bishop Tuttle, of Utah, by commencing to build a church of his order at Logan, where the Mormons have presented him with the most eligible site in their town for its location.

Assuredly, this manifests a kindly feeling between those who differ so widely in form and belief. It is a liberality that will astonish people who have credited all the stories of Mormon exclusiveness and tyranny. So the stone-quarry furnishes material for the worship of God to Mormon and Gentile alike.

Among the prominent Mormons interested in the road are Bishops Hatch, Sharp, Preston, and Shaw. Hon. Moses Thatcher, and Judge Smith. The latter gentleman, who resides in Brigham City, has thirty sons employed in its construction.

At this flourishing town of Hampton is also the dairy, established by Brigham Young. Last year it produced over one hundred and fifty tons of some of the best cheese in the world. Seventeen miles further north is Mendon. Between this and the adjoining town of Logan, Brigham Young owns one of the finest farms of the West, comprising ten thousand acres of very superior land, and stocked at the present time with six hundred head of cattle and large flocks of sheep, selected from the choicest breeds.

The population of this beautiful valley is nearly twenty thousand. The main product is grain, of which seven hundred and fifty thousand bushels were harvested last year. Most of the wheat has been shipped to San Francisco, and thence around Cape Horn to England. The farmers have realized one dollar per bushel, and, with the expectation of a greater ratio of profit, double the amount will be raised in the ensuing year.

From Logan the road is by this time running twenty miles beyond, through several small towns, to Franklin. Fifteen miles still further north, on its proposed continuation, a coal-mine has been recently opened. Timber is abundant in the cañons a few miles from the track. With all these advantages, present and prospective, the success of the " Utah Northern " is assured. As the government directors of the " Union Pacific " have stated in their official report, it will be one of the most important feeders of that great and prosperous national highway. It will eventually extend through Idaho and reach Montana, thus saving the present tedious stage-travel of five hundred miles.

Cache Valley, through which our route now lay, is, like that of Salt Lake, bounded on the east and

west by high ranges of snow-topped mountains, and
about the same width of twenty-five miles.   Bear
River runs through its entire length and empties itself
into Great Salt Lake.   Logan, a town of three thousand inhabitants, is the capital of this county.

We arrived there in the evening, and were conducted in a carriage to the comfortable and well-
furnished house of Brigham Young, Jr., the elder
brother of my companion, and met with a very cor-
dial reception.   The Logan wife of our host is a
handsome and agreeable lady, as is also another of
his wives whom I afterwards met at Salt Lake.   A
daughter of the latter, a charming and accomplished
girl of seventeen, was just now staying with her
"aunt" at Logan.   This was my first night beneath
a Mormon roof.   I was struck by the exact obser-
vance of religious forms which I afterwards found
everywhere prevalent.   In all their houses, among the
rich and the poor, and in the country hotels, a bless-
ing always precedes each meal, and there are always
morning and evening prayers.   When I retired to my
room, instead of the prayer-book accompanying the
Bible, which I often see in the houses of my Episcopalian friends, I found the Book of Mormon placed
upon it.   I do not think, however, that the Mormons
themselves read this book very much.   But they are
astonishing biblical students.   They can quote Scrip-

ture from end to end.   They did this in a way that
amazed the Rev. Dr. Newman, and they are per-
petually flinging texts at your head, especially such as
they claim confirmatory of their peculiar doctrines.

Brigham Young, Jr., is a portly gentleman of about
forty years.   He is already one of the twelve apostles,
and is aspiring, on the death of his father, to succeed
to the presidency of the Church.   The elder Brigham
is known to favor his claims.   It is natural that he
should desire to perpetuate the priesthood in his own
line.   As his wishes are laws with his people, the ambition of his son will doubtless be gratified, although
there are many abler and more experienced men who
might be selected.

Young Brigham has had the character of being
rather " fast " in his earlier days, but, as matrimony
is said to sober a man down, he has already had
enough of it to bring him down to a fair standard of
sobriety.   The changes which will soon come over
the Church, in the abolition of polygamy and in the
modification of other peculiar doctrines, will probably
render the task of governing lighter for the son than
it has been for his father.

On the next day Mr. J. W. Young and I left Logan
in a wagon for Franklin, a distance of twenty miles
north.   Our road was bordered by well-cultivated
farms, all under the system of irrigation and ex-

ceedingly productive. Every little settlement is a bishopric, and Franklin, a town of one thousand inhabitants, is under the keeping of Bishop Hatch, to whose house we drove on arrival, and were kindly received. This bishop is the husband of three wives. He construes the Scripture injunction that a " bishop shall be the husband of one wife," as an unfinished command, the words " at least " having been omitted or implied. As it takes two houses to hold his large family, I was not surprised that my friend and myself were assigned the same room ; but the occupancy of the same bed was a phase of civilization to which our eastern ideas are not much accustomed.

In the night we were awakened by a cry that the Indians were stealing the horses on the prairies, and this made quite an excitement, all the settlement turning out except Mr. Young and myself, who were guests ; and, moreover, our horses were safe under the sheds. The Indians got off with half a dozen animals, and made good their escape. These fellows are getting to be very troublesome. The other day they killed the driver of a Montana stage, not far from here, and robbed the passengers and express.

In the morning I went on a survey with Mr. Young and our host, to the ground where it is proposed to continue the Utah Northern Railroad, now terminating at Logan. Coming to a spot by the banks of

Bear River that could be traversed only on foot, a lad and I were left to guard the animals. We accordingly picketed them, and, placing our guns within reach, amused ourselves by trying to catch some trout; but we caught no fish, and shot no Indians.

We all returned at evening to spend another night with the bishop, who gave me a parting benediction in his morning prayer, when he implored " that the eyes of thy servant who is providentially with us may be opened to the light of thy salvation." Then saying good-by to him and to my pleasant companion, Mr. Young, whose business called him back to Salt Lake, I proceeded up the valley, driven by one of his men, to Soda Springs.

The road was varied by hill and dale, though generally in the bottom of the Cache Valley. We passed the first night at Johnson's ranch. Johnson is a queer old Mormon. He is not a practical polygamist. His means would not warrant it. He has been a missionary to Australia and the Sandwich Islands, where he professed to have made many converts to the faith, and now has retired to this lonely spot, where he seems to do nothing but raise a few cattle and drink a good deal of whiskey. He made us comfortable after the manner of Bishop Hatch, but I fancied still less turning in with a wagon-driver than with a gentleman. There is a large, warm sulphur spring close by the cabin, in which we both bathed before retiring, and this partially reconciled me to the arrangement. Mr. Johnson's neighborhood is infested by rattlesnakes, which form the only excitement of the place. Soon after we left, on the next morning, we killed two of the reptiles and heard the music of a dozen of them in the bushes.

Passing two or three large cattle ranches on our way, it was just at sunset when, leaving an extinct volcano on our left, we turned the base of the eastern mountains in a gorge where the Bear River makes its exit, and our path wound round into the beautiful Soda Valley that here begins its northerly inclined plane, and follows it up for fifty miles.

While the seasons are so mild in the lower valleys, here there is a snow embargo for four or five months, and often for weeks at a time there is no communication with the outside world, excepting on snow-shoes.

CHAPTER III.

THE little village of Soda Springs is eighty-five miles from the terminus of the railroad at Logan, and about two hundred miles in a direct line from Salt Lake City. Although a Mormon settlement, it is within the limits of Idaho. One of these days, when the railroad is completed, its mineral waters will infallibly make it a place of great resort, but now it is simply a collection of twenty log-houses, one of which is termed a hotel.

Some "hotels" I have seen in the wilds of Africa, the plains of India, the slums of Constantinople ; but the "Hotel Sterrit" of Soda Springs is the meanest building of that description into which I ever crept. Sterrit himself is a Mormon, and his energies seem to be directed to raising a numerous family, and making his boarders pay for it by getting nothing in return for their money. Nevertheless, I spent a fortnight there, and I know that I can attribute my health to

HOTEL STERRIT.

the waters, for food, of which there was none, could have had nothing to do with it.

Of these springs I cannot speak too highly. After having visited Saratoga, Carlsbad, Kissingen, and Vichy, I can honestly say that there is more virtue in these springs than in all of the others. What is wanting to the invalid is the excitement always found in the music and the company at fashionable watering-places ; but these deficiencies are counterbalanced by the pure air, and the abundant amusement of hunting and fishing. These two are pleasurable means of supporting life.

There are some warm springs that may be used advantageously for bathing, but the most remarkable are the cool soda-fountains, of which there are several. These come bubbling up clear as crystal from the ground in great pools, and are delicious to the taste, and full of carbonic-acid gas as the soda drawn from the druggists' siphons. Soda, magnesia, and iron are their principal ingredients, and I do not know of an individual having tried them for digestive difficulties who has not been benefited by their use. By and by they will surely find their way, like Congress water, all over the world, and will meet with equal favor.

The climate is variable, yet healthy : an elevation of eight thousand feet above the level of the sea renders it very cool in the morning. The glass at an early hour often indicates forty degrees, rising till the hottest part of the day—this is at four in the afternoon—when it frequently stands at ninety degrees, and then the air grows cool again in the evening. The atmosphere is so rarefied that we at first found breathing difficult after slight exercise ; but one gradually becomes accustomed to this. High as we were, there were mountains all around two or three thousand feet higher, and covered with perpetual snow.

There were very few guests at the Hotel Sterrit, as most people who come prefer to camp out and do their housekeeping out-of-doors. Several members of Brigham Young's family were passing their summer here, among others the lady who is supposed to be his favorite wife, Mrs. Amelia. She is a very pleasant, agreeable, and rather pretty woman, of perhaps thirty-five years, and it is said that she has a greater influence over her husband than all the other sixteen ladies combined. He is now building for her a magnificent house in Salt Lake City; that is more than he has done for any of the others, and this partiality seems to justify what is said of her power.

To make time pass pleasantly while " undergoing a course of the waters," I bought an Indian pony with his accoutrements of saddle, bridle, cantinas or saddle-bags, etc., for the sum of sixty-five dollars. Little Dick was a good purchase, for I not only rode him here daily on hunting and fishing excursions, but afterwards hundreds of miles over the plains and mountains of Utah. The untiring beast would make his sixty miles, and in one instance eighty miles, in a day, and be always fresh for the morrow. The six-hundred-dollar thoroughbred that I ride in the Park is not worth half the money at which I valued little Dick, who finally was sold for forty dollars when I came away.

The Utah Northern Railroad being now completed to Franklin from its new starting-point at Ogden, Soda Springs is within an easy journey of a week from New York, by the New York Central, Lake Shore, Chicago and North-western, Union Pacific, and Utah Northern Railroads. The whole cost of travel over these various roads, including sleeping-car comforts, need not exceed one hundred and fifty dollars. A new and comparatively comfortable hotel will be completed next spring, and doubtless there will then be more "society." But if any reader can be induced by my experience to take his rebellious liver there for satisfactory repairs, and by that of others to have his rheumatic joints made supple, let him not forget his fowling-piece and fishing-rod. He can buy a pony on the spot. These are powerful supplements to the unquestionable virtues of the waters of Soda Springs.

CHAPTER IV.

Soda Springs, *August* 4.

I HAVE just returned from a very pleasant wagon-trip to Fort Hall.

This post is on the Indian Reservation in Idaho Territory, fifty-five miles west from Soda Springs. In company with Mr. Mansfield, a gentleman who was on his way to Montana, and a driver, I left here after breakfast on Saturday morning, in a double-spring wagon. It was a very cool day at the commencement, the mercury standing at thirty-eight degrees, and we found our overcoats quite comfortable; but before the afternoon had passed we dispensed with them, and would have been glad to "sit in our bones."

The first part of the journey was over a wide plain with high ranges of mountains on each side, the snow still resting on their summits. It was much like the valley of Salt Lake. During the forenoon we shot half a dozen grouse and some pigeons, and at noon, when about half the distance, camped by the side of a stream where the willows made a pleasant shade, and, turning our horses loose, lighted a fire, picked some of our birds and fried and roasted them, having good appetites for our meal.   Near by were camped some drovers, with a herd of five hundred cattle, bound up to Montana.   The men were a rough but lively set, not choice in language or manners.

In the afternoon we started again, when the road began to ascend through a cañon to the "Summit."   It was very pretty, although entirely devoid of trees, of which there were none upon the whole road excepting the willows on the side of the brooks, and an occasional dwarf cedar.   Neither was there a single habitation of any kind.   Our course was nearly due west.   Just before sunset we reached the summit, and then came upon a magnificent view, as we looked down over a lot of small mountains and valleys upon the immense plain through which run the Blackfoot and Snake Rivers.   There was a light mist rising from the waters, which gave the appearance of a wide blue sea, and the little hills intervening looked like islands on its bosom.   The high, distant mountains beyond were clearly defined, and were of a lapis-lazuli blue, so beautiful that it cannot be described.   It was a view, in many respects, like that of the bay of Rio

from the Serra of Petropolis. It was still before our
eyes as we drove rapidly down into the valley, and we
watched the changing hues of the skies and of the
landscape till evening covered them from our sight.

Soon after dark we arrived at the fort. There is,
properly, no fort: there is a parade-ground enclosed
by the buildings serving for quarters. At the upper
end are three neat cottages, one occupied by the
captain and doctor, who mess together, another as an
office, and the largest by Lieut. King and his family.
We had a note of introduction to the latter gentleman.
At the opposite end of the parade are the stables and
sutler's shop. On one side of the square are the
soldiers' barracks and wash-houses; on the other the
commissary stores and hospital. In the middle is the
flag-staff, from which " The Star-Spangled Banner
for ever shall wave," to the terror of evil-doers,
whites, Indians, and half-breeds. That is Fort Hall.

The post is maintained not so much by way of
precaution in case of trouble with the Indians, as for
protection of them against the encroachments of the
whites. It may be assumed that in nine cases out of
ten, as has been clearly proved even in the Modoc
war, hostilities are commenced by the settlers, trap-
pers, or miners. On this Reservation are one thousand
five hundred of the Bannock tribe. They are a lazy,
inoffensive set of beings. They are fed and cared for

by the government on the economical principle that it is cheaper to feed them than to fight them. Lieut. King, who has had a long experience on the frontier, understands their character perfectly, and has admirably succeeded in making the government feared and respected not only by the Indians, but by those wretches among the whites who would rob and otherwise maltreat them if they were not thus restrained.

As we drove to the door of Mr. King it was pleasant to see two ladies, neatly dressed, sitting upon the piazza. We received a hearty welcome from the lieutenant, and were at once introduced to his wife and her friend, Miss McCrea. They were young and pleasing, refined and intellectual women. We felt the contrast of this society as compared with that of Soda Springs. It is so seldom that a visitor comes along, that Lieut. King and his family, Capt. Vivian and Dr. Boone, seemed as glad to see us as we were to see them. We declined their offer of supper, as we had just made a meal of the remains of our dinner; and, after sitting with them an hour or two, were shown to a large airy room with two beds, faultless linen, and everything as neat as wax, Lieut. King apologizing because he could do no better than to put us in one room. An apology to people who had been living at Sterrit's Hotel! We slept soundly, of

course.   In the morning we had a superb breakfast,
French coffee, cream, muffins, eggs, trout, chicken,
etc., etc.   Well, that was another contrast to Sterrit's
fried bacon and Japan tea.

After that we were shown around, visiting all the
buildings and stables.   The Doctor was very proud
of his hospital and dispensary.   He said they were
in such perfect order because he never had any use
for either of them.   Altogether, including the soldiers
and hangers-on, there are only eighty people at the
fort.   The ladies seem quite contented.   Mrs. King
has a little girl four years old, and one of the soldiers
is its nurse.   The Corinne and Montana daily stage
passes within twelve miles of the fort, and they send
over every day for the mail.   I found on their tables
all the magazines and daily New York papers, and
read a *Herald* a week old.   When I left, Lieut. King
and the Doctor gave me a lot of them, including June
and July *Atlantic*.   What prizes to bring back to
Soda Springs !

Mr. Mansfield being bound up to Montana, Lieut.
King sent him over to meet the stage, in the forenoon.   They would have kept us both a week if we
could have stayed.   I never met more hospitable people ; but I wanted to be on the best shooting-ground
in the morning early, and so, after an excellent lunch,
bade them good-by.   In September, Lieut. King and

the Doctor, with ten men, are going on a scouting expedition to Soshone Falls on Snake River, some four hundred miles hence. These falls are said to be superior to Niagara. They urged us to join them most enticingly. It would be a horseback journey, and if they were to go now I should most certainly accept the invitation.

We left on our return at three o'clock in the afternoon, and after passing over the summit, where we had another view like that of the preceding day, descended on this side to the banks of the Port Neuf, a little stream, where we camped for the night, having shot two grouse on the way, from which we made our supper. Here we lay down under the wagon, turned our horses loose, and hauled our rugs over us, anticipating sleep. But this was sadly disturbed by millions of mosquitoes. They got in under the shawls and bit; but the worst of it was their ceaseless music. However, they bit and sung us to sleep at last. At five this morning we harnessed our animals and started. Soon after sunrise we shot eight grouse, and then it began to rain ; but we covered ourselves up as well as we could and drove rapidly along, reaching Soda Springs at noon.

Just before arrival we passed the camp of Mr. Shirley, who was on one of his trips from the West to " the East," as he calls Laramie, Cheyenne, and the towns along the U. P. railroad. He was driving a herd of twelve hundred horses in that direction. We stopped for a few minutes to "talk horse" with him. "Big business and small profits" is my motto, said Shirley. That means, small profits are the biggest. "Now one of you Down-Easters will buy a hoss and trade him for another, and keep on one-hoss trading and make fifty dollars out of it. Well, I'm content to make ten dollars a head, and that's $12,000 for my trip. It will take me three months, and then I'll try it over again." On my way home I met Shirley at a railroad station some eight hundred miles east of where I met him here. He had but a hundred horses left and had done better than he had hoped, for his twelve thousand dollars profit had already accrued to him.

CHAPTER V.

IT was my intention to have waited a few days and then to have gone to Cariboo on my pony, but the next morning a party of three men came up from Logan, and so urged me to take a seat with them in their wagon that I accepted their invitation.

Having exchanged their horses for a mule-team, we left Soda Springs at ten in the morning. We soon found that the mules were wretched substitutes for the horses, but as the ground to Warmack's ranche, fifteen miles distant, on the Blackfoot, was quite level, we cudgelled them along till we arrived there and dined. After dinner we caught a few trout, and then started to complete the remaining thirty-five miles. We got on over the first half of the distance, which was on a level road, tolerably well. Then our real troubles began. The mosquitoes attacked us in swarms, the ground mired, the mules balked, we got set in the sloughs, and it began to rain in torrents.

The road was now all up-hill through a dark-wooded cañon, the moon only occasionally breaking through the clouds. So we travelled along, sometimes by her light, and at others by the aid of lightning flashes, often stopping in utter bewilderment, and unwilling to camp in the rain, especially as my companions had a positive engagement to arrive in the morning. One of the mules was particularly lazy and obstinate, continually lying down in the road, and obliging us to club him to get him on his feet.

Fortunately our driver was an energetic fellow. He whipped, clubbed, swore, and yelled steadily at the " cussed " team. His swearing was something stupendous and perfectly exhaustive of Heaven, Earth, and Hell, and of all their inhabitants. No words could do it justice. But the climax was reached when it began to snow thickly, and some of us were straying along ahead of the wagon through a deep gorge in the hills. All at once, within ten rods of us, a grizzly set up a tremendous growl that drowned out the swearing of our driver. We just dropped on all fours and crawled back to the wagon, into which we tumbled rather quickly. We had only a double-barrelled shot-gun with us, and all of us, of course, had pistols; but these small-arms were not much against a grizzly, and we did not intend to use them unless he attacked us. So we drove along until we came to the place where he was.

When he heard the wagon coming he trotted out within two or three rods of us. Then our driver set up a yell and commenced to swear in a style that exceeded all his previous efforts, and actually scared the grizzly so that it fairly made him turn tail and put for the woods. Well, we were glad !

Onward we staggered in the rain, mud, and darkness—sometimes getting out to belabor the mule, sometimes steadying the wagon from capsizing, until at length, at half-past one o'clock, we came to a log-house, which we were told was " Cariboo." The real name of the town is Keenan City. It contains about a dozen log-houses, including a " saloon," lodging-house, and restaurant, entertainment being furnished on the " European plan."

My companions were not satisfied with having emptied a two-gallon jug of whiskey during the day, it having given out soon after midnight. So they routed out the saloon-keeper, who was also the proprietor of the lodging-house, and took several more drinks. It was consequently after 2 A.M. when we were shown to our " apartment." This was a log-house of one room, twenty by fifteen feet, in which two gentlemen were already sleeping on a shelf under a blanket. Two other double shelves were provided for us. Neither of them had a mattress upon it, but they were furnished with horse-blankets, and pillows were not. I selected the least inebriated of my fellow-passengers for a bedfellow, and turned in after placing my coat and pantaloons on an empty box, using my monkey-jacket for a pillow, and walking to my shelf over the bare ground, for the apartment had no floor. But we were all tired enough to sleep until seven o'clock, when I awoke first and got out of doors.

It was a lovely morning after the storm, and the air was delightfully cool and invigorating. But the wretched, woebegone look of Keenan City! The street was nearly knee-deep with mud, and the miners were already wading through it to their work, with their picks, shovels, and pans on their backs. I went to the restaurant and found it was kept by a Scotchman and his wife, an Englishwoman. It was an agreeable disappointment to find it very neatly arranged, and my breakfast of toast and fresh butter, and a tender beefsteak with potatoes, was well cooked, and served. It was far better than anything I had had at Soda Springs.

I met Jeff Davis at the table—not Jeff the rebel, but Jeff the teamster whom I knew at Soda Springs, and who is well known all over this country. After breakfast, Jeff, who has somehow taken a great fancy to me, proposed a walk to the placer diggings, a mile or two outside the city limits. I was very glad to go with him, as he is a very intelligent man, and was able to explain all about the working of the placers.

The men were busily employed in the gulch when we arrived. This gulch is away back in the pine forest, and the sight is very romantic. The men were at their work, and near by among the trees several log-cabins, tastily decorated with spruce boughs, and some very spruce young women too, the wives and daughters of the miners, around them.

The process of placer-mining is hydraulic, a strong stream of water being turned on to wash away the banks of dirt and then running through wooden flumes, in the bottom of which the gold settles and is afterwards removed.

Besides these works there are some owned by poor men and Chinamen, who "pan out" the gold in the primitive way. I borrowed a pan and was not very successful, getting only a few specks of dust for my trouble. Indeed, little is done by this method now, those who simply "pan" rarely getting more than two or three dollars per day.

In the afternoon Mr. Brown, my landlord, invited me to go with him to the top of the mountain and see the place where he had been successfully prospecting for quartz-gold. My friend Jeff offered me the use of one of his mules. Brown and I accordingly started at two o'clock, and ascended towards the mountain through what would have been a magnificent forest if a recent fire had not sadly marred its beauty. Still there was a great deal of beauty left. There was no trail, and we were obliged to pick our way through thick underbrush and over hundreds of fallen trees. Cariboo is about two thousand feet higher than Soda, so that it is some ten thousand feet above the level of the sea. The mountain is fifteen hundred feet above the level of the town.

After ascending five hundred feet we came to patches of snow. Above them it was beautifully green with pines and grass, and just where gold was "struck," halfway to the summit, there was a great, wide, grassy lawn, looking as if it had been laid out by a landscape-gardener. On the edge of this, among the pines, were the huts of the prospecters, made of bark and pine-boughs, and having a very tasty appearance.

It was only three weeks since these quartz-mines were discovered, and the ore had not yet been thoroughly assayed. But they are probably very rich, and are likely to be the original source of the deposits found in the gulches. Very little work has been done in them as yet. After looking at the specks of gold in the broken quartz, and wishing that I owned the

mountain, I determined to get upon the top of it and
tread all its gold under my feet.   I found a very
intelligent young Scotchman, a Glasgow lad, among
the prospecters, and he went with me.   It was tedious climbing over loose rocks, and through deep
snow ; but we accomplished it at last, and were amply
rewarded by such a view as no pen can describe.
We were on the highest peak of the range, and looked
down upon lesser mountains of snowy summits, and
over them all beyond the valleys near us, into valleys
in the far distance, tracing the Snake and Blackfoot
Rivers for at least a hundred miles, and taking in on
all sides everything that could be seen without let or
hindrance from intervening objects as far as the eye
could reach in the clear atmosphere on this brilliant
afternoon.   The extent was so great that even the
beauties and grandeur of the Yosemite were eclipsed
by the magnificent panorama.   We descended rapidly,
sliding over the snow-patches down to the green, where
Mr. Brown was waiting with the mules ; and bidding
my friendly Scotchman good-by, we started for the
town below.   It was nearly dark before we arrived,
but our faithful animals carried us safely down.

Thursday, M., Aug. 6th.—Early this morning Jeff
turned me out, saying, " Hurry up with your breakfast ; the mules are all ready, and you must go with
us over beyond the mountain and see some of the

other quartz-leads ; it is a pretty rough ride and it will take all day."

My toilet was made in something less than three minutes, and after breakfast we trotted out of the valley and took the mountain-trail, which soon was lost in the thick copses and fallen trees. Our way was longer and even rougher than that of yesterday. There were almost perpendicular descents into ravines, and away up more than a thousand feet above the valley, we crawled along on the side-hill like flies on the edge of a teacup. Horses could not have held on ; but these sure-footed mules, bracing themselves upwards, picked their way in a most wonderful manner. It was far safer to remain on their backs than it would have been to dismount, for a single misstep would have sent one down below without stopping for breath.

"Your mule is responsible for you," said Jeff. " Just don't touch the reins, but look at the prospect " —and so I did and soon forgot all care for myself in the contemplation of the beautiful and sublime scenery. Below us was an immense basin-shaped valley, carpeted with the greenest grass, and figured with patches of giant pines, looking like shrubs, beneath us. Over beyond, range upon range, were clearly-defined mountains of different shades of dark granite to the faintest blue in the far distance.

In this way we rode fifteen miles in six hours, when we came upon a party of prospecters known to Jeff and Mr. Perkins, my other companion. In the early part of our ride we had come through flocks of mountain-grouse. They were so tame that we shot them with our pistols from the saddle, and brought along a lot of young chickens with us. We camped at 1 P.M. with Thompson and Graham and another man, the prospecters who had just discovered a new quartz-lead, from which they expect of course to make their fortunes.

Introduction and drinks were in order as necessary accompaniments, and it is only by falling back on absolute temperance or rather total abstinence that I have escaped being drunk half the time, and being poisoned for life, since I have been in Cariboo. Messrs. Thompson and Co. made us welcome, and offered us all their hospitalities.

They admitted that they were not so well " fixed " as they might be. They had been living there a week, but had not even a tent for a covering, and had lost their axe, so that they could not cut pine-boughs to make a hut; but they had chosen a romantic spot among the thick evergreens. Within a few rods of them was a large snow-bank from which water enough melted for their supply, and deliciously cool it was. But they had plenty of flour, bacon, and whiskey for food and stimulant and of blankets for sleep. They were as healthy-looking a set of men as I ever saw, notwithstanding their coarse diet and bad liquor; for it was seasoned with hope and bright anticipations.

If I was asked what miners lived upon I should answer, "Whiskey and hope." As to the former, I would prefer having the value of what is drunk, to having all the gold that is panned in Cariboo; for the miners spend all their gold-dust for whiskey, and are still in debt for it. As to hope, they are always living, and that joyfully, on "great expectations." So now the bottle went round, and then we made a fire and picked our chickens.

In the meantime one of Thompson's men "started a bake." Having the yeast already prepared from a powder, he mixed the flour in a frying-pan, and in less than fifteen minutes turned out a great cake of bread that any epicure would have pronounced most excellent. By this time we had prepared half a dozen grouse and cut them up for "a fry" with bacon. Our entertainers gave us some tea, and we all sat down under a great fir-tree and made a hearty and sociable meal. Mr. Morgan was an old salt, and had been a mate in the Black Ball line. We had sea-yarns for our dessert, and laughing for nuts and raisins.

After they had all "had a smoke" and some more whiskey, we went to see the new quartz-lead near by.

DINNER PARTY ON MT. PISGAH.

Some of it was decayed mineral which yielded on being washed in a pan about thirty cents' worth of gold in ten minutes. By this rough process, however, half of it was lost. I was quite satisfied that they had " struck a good thing," if the vein is not all surface. But it may go to a great depth and may not. From each side of the great mountain already described runs a stream through valleys into the plain below. In these valleys, one of which holds Cariboo, are the placer diggings, all along by the side of the streams washing down the gold.

The miners have heretofore been contented with these deposits, for they are rich and sure. But they naturally supposed that the particles of gold came from a quartz source, and that this source could not be elsewhere than in the mountains whence the streams take their rise. Hence all the present excitement and prospecting for quartz-gold. The quartz-mines, if rich, are generally immensely so, but they are much more uncertain than the placers, and require a great deal more capital to work them. I should rather take my chance with the placers.

We " packed in " a lot of quartz on a mule, which Thompson sent back. While saddling our animals one of them got loose and took the mountain to himself. Jeff and another man " put for him " on muleback, and the rest of us " corraled " him on foot. It was a most exciting chase, and I never saw such riding as this. The runaway and his pursuers galloped and wheeled on the edge of precipices, among bushes, trees, rocks, and over loose stones which rolled from under their feet into the chasms below, the riders shouting, yelling, and swearing at the chase in the wildest and most horrible style, keeping it up for nearly a half-hour. By that time we had surrounded the mule and corraled him. Then bidding adieu to our hospitable friends, we started on our way home, travelling over the same ground on which we had come, and shooting some more grouse.

As we came over the divide we witnessed a most glorious sunset, the last rays shooting up through the valleys, and brightening with gold the clouds that hung between the mountains, making a splendid contrast with the cold gray peaks. We were at home at eight o'clock.

Mr. Perkins, who I should have said is the merchant of Cariboo, invited Jeff and myself to take tea with him. His log-cabin on the outside is like all the rest, but on entering there was an air of neatness of which certainly none of the others could boast. In fact, there was a woman in the house, and a very lady-like young woman is Mrs. Perkins. She had muslin curtains for her windows. She had a sewing-machine in one corner of the room, and in the middle of it she had a table set for herself and husband, on which she speedily put two more plates. It was spread with a spotlessly clean cloth, clean napkins in rings, a nice stoneware tea-equipage, with plated-forks and teaspoons, and even a butter-knife ! After a good supper, the gentlemen adjourned to the saloon, where we played high-low-jack, the favorite game in these parts.

I had a bed, or rather a board, to myself last night, and thought this fortunate, as indeed it was. After breakfast, the order of the day was for Jeff to break in a bucking horse. Before he was fairly seated, the first buck threw him " higher than a kite ; " but he calls himself " a wiry old cuss," and he was not much hurt. He was on the horse again in a minute, and then commenced an equestrian exhibition that would have astonished Rarey. Such mad leaping and plunging is not often seen. The animal stood on his hind legs one moment, and at the next his tail pointed to the zenith, but Jeff sat as if glued to the saddle. Then down he went on his side and rolled over on his back, Jeff sliding off as he went down, and jumping on again as he rose. Down again and over and over went the horse, his rider always avoiding being rolled upon, and while he plunged never starting his trousers from the saddle.

For two hours at least this game was kept up, till

the horse had fairly bucked himself out and had sweated himself weak.   Then Jeff took off the saddle and bridle, and putting on the halter, jumped upon his back and rode him up and down the street.   After a while he dismounted, faced his conquest, and looking him in the eye, remarked, with considerable expletive earnestness, "You may buck some other fellow, but I don't calculate you will ever buck me again!"   We were to have gone to "Iowa Valley" to see a new placer claim on this day, but Jeff owned himself too much used up with the exercise he had had, to take a twenty-mile ride.   So we postponed it till the morrow.

After dinner, Mr. Perkins invited me to take a ride with his wife down the cañon.   He put her on a quiet, ambling pony, and gave me an elegant gray horse he had just purchased and which he did not think would buck.   After what I had seen this morning, I clinched my knees to the saddle in anticipation of a contingency, but was agreeably disappointed, and we had a very pleasant ride of about twenty miles, partly on the road and partly over the hills on bridle-paths, coming down at sunset, enjoying a view like that of the evening before.

JEFF ON A BUCKING HORSE.

CHAPTER VI.

ON the morning of August 9th there was a lively time corraling the animals, but they were finally roped in, and we started for " Iowa City." This important town is situated in a valley on the other side of the mountain, distant from Cariboo seven or eight miles. There is nominally a wagon-road for all the distance, but at least one-half of it is merely a trail.

Jeff was mounted on his wild horse of yesterday's performance ; but to-day he was gentle as a kitten. I had the same horse I had ridden the day before. The road was principally through the " burnt district " of the pine forest, and had a gloomy look about it ; but as we began to ascend the cañon, we rode among groves of green pines, pleasingly contrasting with the first part of the route. All along the banks of the stream were the different placer claims being worked by gangs of miners. Some of them were operated by hydraulic pressure, but most of them were worked on a very small scale.

We stopped at the residence of Patrick Gallagher, Esq., and found that gentleman about to dine with his family, consisting of a large dog, a small cat, and a pig. "Bedad, but ye're wilcome, and so is the gintleman wid ye, Misther Jeff," exclaimed Mr. Gallagher; "me dinner is jist ready, and here's a chair apace." With that he shoved two empty boxes towards the shelf serving for a table. "Divil a dhrop of whiskey have I," said our entertainer, and I was not sorry to hear it, because it was such a rare thing to get an introduction to a gentleman without a drink. "But here's an illigant pace of boiled beef, and potaties and bread for ye, and there's wather for ye, if ye know the taste of it."

Mr. Gallagher had two knives and one fork for his table service. "The fork is aisy divided," he said, "for there's three prongs to it, and that's one apace, but be me sowl it bothers me to share round the knives!" However, we managed to make a very hearty meal, notwithstanding deficiencies of table service. As nearly as I could measure the one-roomed house by the eye, it was ten feet by six. This, of course, included eating-room, sleeping-room, kitchen, and hall.

After dinner we went out to see his claim, which

he, in connection with three partners, worked with hydraulics. He said they had averaged ten dollars a day apiece this summer, and expressed himself as "contineed." Well he might be.

I really could not find "Iowa City," although I was assured that we had been there. Here and there, within the distance of half a mile, there were some log-cabins, in all perhaps half a dozen, and these must have been in the different wards of Iowa City. The last place to which we came was the residence of William Clemens, Esq., the head man of the place ; there we alighted, tied our horses to trees, and then went with Mr. Clemens to see his claim. To arrive at it one must go on foot, by a wild, shaded path through the pine woods. On the way we gathered a great many whortleberries, as they are called here, but they are only so in the appearance of the bushes, the berries growing larger than the eastern whortleberries, of a dark purple color, and being slightly acid, very pleasant to the taste.

The claim of Mr. Clemens is in the bed of what was a stream some thousands of years ago, and the developments thus far have equalled his expectations. To judge from the soil around it, no one unacquainted with mining would have imagined that below it had ever been a river-course. The intuitive perception of these otherwise ignorant men, which enables them to prospect successfully, is a mystery to me. They are not scientific, but they are very practical mineralogists.

Returning to the cabin of Mr. Clemens and resting awhile, we mounted our horses, and came back to Cariboo.

It was Saturday night, and the little "camp" was somewhat more than ordinarily noisy, profane, and drunk. Several wagons had arrived and completed a journey of many weeks, perhaps months, from the "States." The women were busy around their camp-fires preparing their meals, while their husbands were carousing in the "saloon," and they all felt happy in their different ways. In a day or two they will have prospected and selected claims, living in the meanwhile in and under their wagons, as they have done on their journey, and in a week or two they will have built and furnished their future homes—future—till in a future more remote some of them will occupy brown-stone fronts in Chicago and New York. Will they be happier then, when dizzy at the summit of their ambition, than they now are at the base of the mountain, toiling cheerfully in the ascent, and fortunately ignorant how bleak and barren is the pinnacle beyond which they cannot go?

What would this life of ours be without the future that is in it, even in this world? As we advance in years this future becomes more contracted, but still there is always till death a little of it, and it is in the contemplation and magnifying of this little that we have our chief stimulus for exertion. It seems to me that people are most happy when about half-way up the mountain. They have then plenty of anticipations for the future, and a pleasing remembrance of the past, while they are not too high for the beautiful things around them to be dimmed by distance.

A Sabbatarian would have been disgusted with the manner the Sunday has been observed in Cariboo. There is not a Bible or Prayer-book, or even a Book of Mormon, in the place. Here we are outside the pale of the Mormon and all other churches. But the people do not forsake the assembling of themselves together for the enjoyment of Sunday after their own style. The grand drunk of last night has been continued and intensified since morning. To-day even the Chinamen, who are the soberest and best-behaved of the population, come to the bar with their bottles for " lilly whiskey." In this respect they have on Sunday embraced Cariboo Christianity. On the first day of the week the faro-table is more patronized than on any other.

I suppose the services were continued in the afterpart of the day as in the forenoon, but I was not a witness, for I got on horseback after dinner and crept up to the top of the mountain to enjoy the magnificent prospect that I have already described. It was as beautiful as before, and much more sublime.

Just before sunset a heavy squall passed from south to north over the chain of mountains to the westward, the sun burying himself in the dark bank, and sending upwards his rays of purple and gold. Then, indeed, "from peak to peak leaped the live thunder," the bright zigzag chains of lightning scarcely giving time for the thunder to roll before they commenced their wild play again ; and this is the way in which one of the mining gentlemen described the scene : " Well, there was a hell of a dust kicked up over yonder this afternoon ! " Fortunately the rain did not reach me, but it was nearly dark when I arrived at the " hotel."

I returned to Soda Springs from Cariboo after one of the quickest rides of fifty miles which I ever enjoyed. Mr. Perkins had a fine mustang he wished to send here, and I was only too glad to embrace the opportunity to ride him down.

The day had been quite cool and cloudy, and for an hour it rained a little ; but the only trouble for me was from the mosquitoes, and for the horse from flies. Of both classes of insects there were myriads. My green veil was white with the one, and the bay hide of the poor horse was black with the other. If I stopped him, or even walked him, he became perfectly frantic ; so I let him go along at his own rattling lope of ten miles an hour.

When clear of the cañon, after having passed the spot where we had encountered the grizzly on our upward journey, I congratulated myself on the remoteness of his lair. Quite easy in my mind as·to any apprehended danger on the prairie, I was startled by such a sudden stop of the horse that I preserved my balance with some difficulty.

No wonder that the animal trembled from head to foot, or that I " felt my heart in my mouth." Directly in front of us, at the distance of a few feet, sat on his haunches a large catamount, with anger in his glowing eyeballs and temper in his expanded bushy tail. I was about to draw my pistol from the holster, when I remembered that it had been discharged the day before and I had forgotten to reload it. Perhaps this was fortunate, for if I had fired and only wounded the animal, the consequences might have been unpleasant to contemplate. I dared not advance unarmed, nor did I dare to turn and run away. After a few seconds of deliberation, I concluded to adopt a medium policy. I then quietly and slowly drew my horse out of the trail into the sage-brush on the right, and my ioy was unspeakable when that intelligent catamount also called to his mind the old rule of " keep to the

right as the law directs," which he obeyed, as soon as
he saw that I complied with it.

After a sufficient détour to avoid him, in case he
should change his pacific determination, I came into
the road again, keeping a bright lookout ahead during the rest of the journey for any intrusive beast.   I
stopped at Warmack's ranch, on the Blackfoot River,
the only house, and consequently the only place on
the road for refreshments for man and beast.   I had
trout, and the horse had oats, and we both dined
well.   I left Cariboo at 10 A.M., passed an hour
and three quarters at Blackfoot, and arrived here at
5 P.M., so that I was but a trifle more than five
hours on the road.   I was now again at the " Hotel
Sterrit," and this writing closes the account of nearly
a week's absence pleasantly passed in a trip to
Cariboo.

There are but few Mormons engaged in the mining
operations at Cariboo.   The genius of the people
does not lie in that direction.   They are almost strict-
ly addicted to agricultural and pastoral pursuits.   Thus
wealth, or rather comfortable independence, is more
equally distributed among them than in most communities.   It is this inculcation by the Mormon
religion, rather than the religion itself, that makes
them a happy and a virtuous people.   There is great
wisdom in the advice given them by Brigham Young,

to be contented with their crops, their flocks, and their herds. They follow it faithfully, and so they do not go to Cariboo.

There are many pretty rides in the neighborhood of Soda Springs. One is well repaid for a visit to the volcano, to the mines, and sulphur lakes, to the mountain cañons, all within easy reach from the village. There are always camps of the Bannock Indians not far from the town, to which these wild, dirty, but harmless vagabonds resort for trade.

Notwithstanding the enactment of strict laws, they do obtain whiskey from the traders in barter for skins and game.

The management of the Utah tribes by the Mormon government while it had supreme control, was greatly to its credit. The Mormons imitated the humane policy of the Pennsylvania Quakers, rather than such a war of extermination as is advocated by Phil Sheridan. This is the General's logic : " They are a miserable set of wretches who must inevitably disappear before the progress of civilization. In the meantime they stand in its way. Therefore, for their own benefit and for that of civilization, the sooner they are cleared out the better."

True enough, all attempts to domesticate and elevate them have been failures. It has been thus from the first settlement of New England, when the

enthusiastic Elliot, after spending years in acquir
ing the language of some of the Massachusetts tribes,
devoted other years to translating the Bible into
their tongue. When the task was accomplished and
the book was printed, nearly all the Indians had
passed away, so that there was never a demand for
the second edition.

The Indian policy of the government is indeed surrounded by difficulties. Perhaps Sheridan's logic,
though cruel, is correct; but the work will be better
accomplished without a resort to wholesale butchery.
The moral force alone of a strong race will overcome
a weak one, unless the weaker is in a condition of
protection amounting to slavery. Thus the negroes
who increased when they were really cared for, however
unjust the system holding them in bondage, now that
they have to fight the battle of life side by side
with white men, must inevitably succumb and disappear. Laziness and carelessness of the future belong
to them and the Indians alike. But they have been
domesticated by slavery, are more congregated, more
attached to localities, and, above all, they are Chris-
tianized. So they will last longer than the Indians.

What, then, shall be our policy? It seems to me
that Lieut. King at Fort Hall expressed it correctly:
"It is cheaper to feed them than to fight them." That
is true, unless we mean by fighting them to extermi-

nate them at once. Humanity forbids this. All that we have to do is to nurse them along until they die a natural death.

If we wish to hasten this, let us encourage the traders, who will bring it about more speedily by the administration of poisonous whiskey. Perhaps those philanthropic gentlemen think they are doing God service by clearing out these Canaanites with a more potent weapon than was put into the hands of Israel. It is well for them to remember that "it must needs be that offences come ; but woe to that man by whom the offence cometh ! "

The craving of Indians for spirituous liquors is insatiable. It is impossible to repress their devilish appetite. The most harmless creatures in the world without whiskey, when it comes in their way they invariably get drunk, not as white men do with different results, but always to quarrel. " Mormon Jack," as they called him, because he was a supposed convert to Mormon Christianity, was a splendidly formed Bannock. He was not only remarkably handsome, but very intelligent. He used to point out the best "trout-holes" and hunting-grounds, and became for me a pleasant companion. One day I missed him. Asking his squaw what had become of him, she replied, "Too much whiskey—too much fight—too much kill." Some scoundrel-trader had sold to Jack and another Indian each a bottle of whiskey. They sat down in a friendly way to drink their liquor. Both, of course, finished their bottles, and then they used them for beating out each other's brains. Nobody thought much of it, for they were —only Indians! But I fancied that Mormon Jack had a soul.

On one of my rides in the direction of Bear Lake, I met a caravan of wagons going west. They were filled with Indians, most of them women, and all of them old or diseased. Asking the white men in charge where they were going, they replied, "To the Reservation. These thieving devils can't support themselves in the settlements, and so we are going to take them there." "What, all the way to Fort Hall?" "Not a bit of it," replied one of the teamsters; "we are only going to carry 'em far enough so they can't get back, and then dump 'em!"

If the poor wretches ever pressed their way to our kind friends at the Post, I am sure they were well cared for; but they were not in a condition to walk fifty miles.

The whites almost universally looking upon the Indians as only troublesome wild beasts to be gotten rid of, we may well believe that their end is not far-distant. By the direct agency of the whites they

are sunk to such a depth of moral degradation, that
intemperance is trivial compared to other vice. No
ingenuity of words can soften a description of their
loathsome and avaricious sensuality. Their wives
and daughters are always in the market for a bottle of
whiskey. I sometimes think that Phil Sheridan is
right, after all. Decidedly the Indian element is not
one of the pleasurable attractions of Soda Springs.

There are enough of other inducements to visit the
place. The really wonderful virtue of the waters, the
pure, unadulterated air, the magnificent mountain scenery, the rides and drives, the hunting and fishing, all
conduce to pleasant pastime and restoration of health.
At only a few hours' journey to the east may be seen
the beautiful Bear Lake, surrounded by pretty villa-
ges and fertile farms—all this region destined, before
many years have elapsed, to become valuable to the
outer world by the means of contemplated railroads.
The summer sojourner need never to be at a loss for
recreation.

I do not agree that the Old World is "played out,"
and that it is entirely superseded by the New; but, if
I may judge from my own experience, there is a certain freshness about this simple normal Western life,
this communion with untamed nature, this study of
mankind as it develops itself indigenously, not arti-
ficially, that far exceeds all that we see in Europe of

polished society, cultivated parks and gardens, old cloisters and musty universities.

And yet, if life be long enough, it is pleasant to see the old and the new of our world.   This may be more nearly accomplished now by any one who has the taste, the means, and the time.   Time! alas that it is so short!   One of the greatest mysteries is that in the old days men lived long when there was so little to see, and that we live so short a life when there is so much before us that we cannot reach!   Why, in that little fragment of Asia, when the horizon of the known earth was bounded by a span, did Methuselah live to the age of nearly a thousand years, and why are we— now that this great, beautiful, glorious world is ever opening to our view—why are we cut down to three-score years and ten? . . Come, little Dick, time is short, and we can stay no longer at Soda Springs.

CHAPTER VII.

I INTENDED to have left Soda Springs earlier in the day, but it was so excessively warm that I deferred my departure until four o'clock in the afternoon. In one hour I was out of the valley of Soda and on the great plain. With the intervention of a few small hills this is a vast level, running all the way down to Salt Lake, where is contained what water there is left of a once large inland sea.

For most of the way the valley is about twenty miles wide. When I came up, we took the road by the base of the eastern mountains that bound it, and now, as I went down, I took that to the west. In either case the route is very beautiful, mountains towering overhead on one side, and clearly outlined and continually changing their colors and shadows on the other.

The pony jogged along very gayly, considering the load of accoutrements which he was obliged to carry most of the way. I missed my gun greatly, for the grouse were starting up in all directions as evening came on, but they were always just out of pistol-shot. So I could only watch them whirring about, and think what a good supper one or two of them would make.

The sunsets are always magnificent in this country. Equally to be admired are the western mountains, when seen from the eastward as the sun drops over them and leaves the clouds upon their summits gilded with silver and gold, and the eastern ranges that then fade into such a lovely blue background.

After proceeding twenty-five miles, I came up with the company and teams of my friend Jeff. They were all camped near Burton's ranch, in a shady spot. Their fires were lighted, and half a dozen men were sitting around preparing supper, while the mules were grazing on the meadow, the long range of covered wagons resembling a military camp. I had hoped that the train had made better progress, as on board of one of the wagons was my sample-bag of mineral which I was anxious should be delivered at Corinne as soon as I arrived there.

"Well, Captain," said Jeff, "I'll tell you what I'll do. I want to go pretty quick myself. I'll let the

boys drive the teams along, and as I have got a horse
here I am taking down to Corinne, I'll borrow a saddle from Burton, and then we'll pack the rocks on
our two horses, and go right along to-morrow morning."

It may readily be believed that the proposal was
gratefully accepted, especially as it would give me the
companionship of Jeff, who knew every ranch and
almost every sage-brush along the road, and moreover is one of the most good-natured fellows in the
world.

" Now, if you like," he said, " you can stop and
camp with us ; but, as it looks like rain, you had
better go on to King's, a mile beyond, where they'll
treat you first-rate. King used to be a Mormon, but
he ain't now. Mrs. King is a nice kind o' woman,
and Tilly, her sister, is a pretty gal. Yes, you'll
like things there under cover, considerable better than
you will here in the rain ; so you go 'long, and I'll
fetch the bag and pack, after you get your breakfast."

Acting on this good advice, I pushed on a mile
further to King's, and found him and his family what
Jeff had represented them to be. Mr. King took
care of Dick and gave him plenty of oats. Mrs.
King and Tilly were anxious to get me a " square
meal ; " but as I preferred bread and milk, they placed
before me some excellent bread and fresh butter, and

a large bowl of cream. That was surely a supper for anybody.

Mr. King is an Englishman. I believe he had been a Mormon conscientiously; certainly it was not for the sake of polygamy. When he was a Mormon he was a bachelor; and now that he is one no longer, he ought to be contented with the one wife that he has. Mrs. King, too, was a Mormoness, or rather, her father was a Mormon. But he and his daughter are now apostates. Tilly says she "don't care nothing about it noways. I'd just as lief marry a Mormon as any other feller; but if I should, and he should open on gitting another wife, that feller or I would have to quit the ranch, and I reckon it would be him that would go!"

In the evening we had a game of high-low-jack—the favorite game alike of Mormon and Gentile—Mr. King and Tilly against Mrs. King and myself, in which our side was whipped, for which I was glad, as it made Tilly so happy. King's house was like all the rest in this country, of logs, and it was small at that, so that they made a bed for me on the floor of the principal room. But it was very comfortable, the sheets were clean, and experience had taught me to sleep anywhere.

In the morning I arose quite early, as I did not wish to put the family to inconvenience. It had rained very hard in the night, but the weather had partially cleared. The sun was climbing up through broken clouds, and making his way over the eastern range. The little household was soon busy, the table was spread with a faultlessly clean cloth, genuine coffee was ground in the mill, hot cakes were baking in the oven, and veal cutlets were snapping in the pan. That was our breakfast, and with the addition of fresh butter and cream, it was "good enough."

By and by Jeff came along with his horse and the bag of mineral. This we divided in two parts, each of us packing about twenty-five pounds. Although I am light enough myself, my cantinas, containing clothes and pistol-holster, and my blankets and overcoat, with the addition of twenty-five pounds of dead weight, were as much as one horse ought to carry. Jeff's animal, however, had more on his back, for Jeff was a heavy man. It was nine o'clock before we started, the teams coming along at the same time. Bidding adieu to my kind hosts, we galloped off and soon left the mules far behind.

We stopped at a house where Jeff had some business with the owner, who, like King, was an apostate. Mrs. Collins, the lady of the mansion, wore no shoes, for absence of which she apologized on the score of poverty. "However," she added, "we're better off now than when we was Mormons; we have got clear of tithing, and that gives a little more money to us, instead of to old Brig."

There was much of truth in that remark. It is a truth that will eventually help to overthrow a great deal of Brigham Young's influence. These apostates are on the confines of Gentile territory. They are apostates because their eyes are opened by their neighbors. When they see them husbanding all their labor for themselves, they soon become averse to giving one-tenth of theirs nominally to the Church of the Latter-day Saints, but really to enrich its leaders. "We did not mind paying tithes," said Mrs. Collins, "so long as we was poor, and didn't have nothin' to pay on. But when we come to have twenty-five cows, I says to Collins, says I, how be we going to give the Church one-tenth of 'em? that's two cows and a half." This arithmetical problem apparently caused them to abandon the faith. If the question had not been proposed until they had owned thirty cows, Mr. and Mrs. Collins might have been yet in the fold.

In answer to the inquiry of Mrs. Collins as to where we proposed to stop for dinner, I said, "at Johnson's ranch," where we passed the night on the upward journey. "Well," she replied, "you won't find nobody to home; Miss Johnson, she's quit." "How is that?" I asked. "Why, she was kind o' discontented like on the whole, what with old Johnson's getting full o' whiskey, and lickin' her "—(be it remembered Johnson had been a Mormon missionary) —"when he was 'round, and when he wan't 'round the Indians gittin' in and threatenin' to scalp her and the children, and the plaguy rattlesnakes that was allers under foot, she had a pretty hard time ; but then I suppose she might have got along if there had been any neighbors, but you know there ain't nobody within twenty miles of 'em. Anyway, she quit, and so Johnson he quit too, and they've moved to Frank-lin."   "You are quite sure of that?" I inquired. "Oh, yes," she answered, "I know it, for no longer ago 'n last night two men stopped here; they was going to put up there, but they found the house shot, and when they looked into the winders they see three or four rattlesnakes kiled up on the floor, so they concluded to come along !"

In two hours' time the heavy clouds that had been gathering at the south burst upon us. As there was no shelter, we had only to put on our overcoats, wrap our blankets about our legs, and "to do as they do in Spain." But it did not last long. As soon as we got through the cañon where the squall came upon us, the weather cleared up, the dust was laid, the air freshened, and we dispensed with our overcoats and jogged merrily on.

Our course lay along the western bank of Bear

River, upon the " bench " above it, and the view was very picturesque of herds of horses and cattle feeding in the meadows below. In one of the droves there were hundreds of horses of all ages and sizes. They were racing about for their own pastime, and seemed to be enjoying themselves amazingly.

Soon after noon we came to Robbins's ranch. We were now in full Mormondom, although scarcely on the confines of Utah.

Mr. Robbins is a family man, and a very good, hospitable man we found him. He and his boys, of whom there was quite a number, took care of our horses, and when we entered the house, his wives and his daughters, of whom there was another number, amply provided for us. Two of the Mrs. Robbins were nursing babies of about the same age. Each Mrs. Robbins was dressed exactly like the other. A third Mrs. Robbins, who did not appear to be troubled with a baby just then, cooked the dinner. Several young Robbins, of ages intermediate between babyhood and youth, were chirping about, roosting on beds inside and on fences without, and Robbins himself strutted about among them all, with the air of a happy husband and father.

He came here from Texas at the time of the rebellion. He is a well-educated and gentlemanly man, and seems to enjoy being a Mormon. He keeps

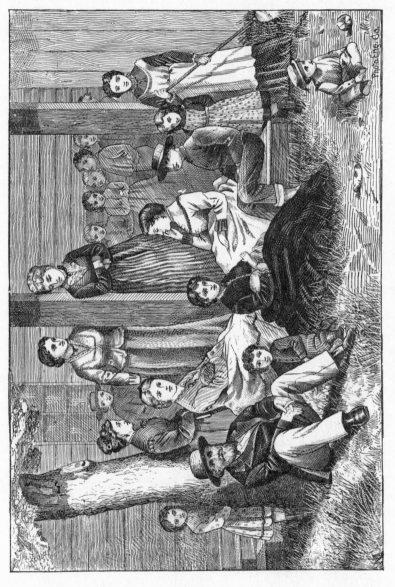

MR. ROBBINS AND SOME OF HIS FAMILY.

what is called a cattle ranch, and has been very successful in raising cattle and children. His cattle lie
down peacefully in green pastures beside the still
waters, and his family lie down peacefully all over the
house on beds and on the floor. To all appearance,
Robbins, his wives, his children, and his cattle, are all
happy. We had a good dinner, clean and well
served. There was little of meat, in which Mormons
do not much indulge, but there was an abundance of
milk, cream, butter, eggs, and vegetables, on which
they mostly live, and live well. Nothing could induce Mr. Robbins to accept any remuneration, but
if I return, I shall remember the children, supposing
my cantinas to hold enough to carry each a stick of
candy !

Mounting our horses again, we went on in the cool
afternoon. As we rode along, Jeff enlivened the journey by his inexhaustible stories of personal adven-
ture and border life.

"I never tried to get married but once," he said,
"and that was to a Mormon gal up here to Logan.
She was jest about the slickest little creetur ever you
see. Fust time I come acrost her was where her folks
and I camped out one night right about here. I
follered on her trail pretty close for six months, and
thought I was going to trap her, sure. She wanted
me to be a Mormon. I wan't partic'ler about that,

but I didn't like to jine any church.   I never did belong to a church or an engine company in the States.
However, I told her finally, as she crowded me, that
I'd swaller Brigham, Tabernacle, and all, for love of
her.   So we got things about fixed, and if she hadn't
gone too fur I might have been a bishop by this
time.

  " But she had an old-maid sister, and she wanted
me to marry that Susan Jane too—that durned, dried-
up, old Susan Jane! 'Emmy,' says I, 'I can't and
I won't!'   So I sot my foot down, and there's where
we split.   You see the old man was kind o' sickly,
and jest as sure as I'd agreed to take Susan Jane,
when he died I would have had to marry the old
woman too!   I hain't hunted after a wife sence.   I've
seen some tol'ble good-lookin' gals down to Salt
Lake, and a good many likely squaws on the Reservation; but the Salt Lake gals are too dressy, and the
squaws ain't dressy enough.   I shan't see nobody
agin like Emmy.   I'd have been a Mormon for her,
but not so much of a one as she wanted me to be.

  " Say what they will about the Mormon gals, I'd
rather have one of 'em than a Gentile.   They ain't
thoroughbreds, I know; but, as a general thing,
they are honest, kind, and true.   They are brought
up to hard work, and they are willing to do their share
on the road.   Take some teams and harness a horse

up with a mare, the mare'll kick up her heels and buck, or else she'll lay back and let the horse do all the work. That's about the way with gals in the States. They're awful pretty there, and they put a nice harness on 'em, but that's no account. They ain't good for nothin' on a drag. Agin, you put some mares in and they'll take their share of the draught right along. These Mormon gals do that. They've read the first chapter of Adam "—(Jeff meant Genesis, and was in error also about the chapter)—" and they know what they was made for. Gals in the States think they was made for playthings, or something worse. They are —— expensive luxuries, anyway.

" There, you don't ask the old woman if the gal can help support you; the old man asks you if you can support his darter. So if a feller falls in love with a gal he's got to buy her, and what's she good for to him after he gits her? What do you call that sort of business but jest what they pitch into the Mormons for? Only it's worse, though 'tis only retail, while theirs is wholesale. I s'pose 'tis kind o' degradin' the way they herd women as they do out here, but it looks to me degradin' for men to jest worship petticoats the way they do in the States."

I had noticed that the back of Jeff's head was marked by a peculiar up-and-down bald spot, while the rest of his skull was covered by a thick crop of red, bushy hair. Emboldened by a companionship that had assumed so much familiarity, I asked him how this singular want of covering was to be accounted for.

"Why, that," he replied, "is where I was scalped by a bar; and that ain't all, he scalped me half-way down my back, as I'll show you to-night. It was— le' me see—six years ago last fall. I was out huntin' deer away to the eastward of Fort Bridger.

"I left camp early one mornin' and tramped pretty much all day without seein' any game, when late in the arternoon I see a big grizzly down in a holler close by. I drawed on him right off, and as I was so close to, I couldn't miss him; so he dropped like a log. I was the durndest fool I ever was in my life, for I walked right up to him without waitin' a minute. But that bar wan't dead. Jest as soon as I touched him he riz right up on his hind legs, and, before I could go for a tree, he put his paw on the top of my head and took har, skin, and all off pretty near clean down to the bone! I had my knife in my hand, for I had drawed it as I went up to him, and I jest had life enough left in me to turn round and jab it into him. I got it straight into his heart, and what with the shot and this lick he was dead then, sure.

"But the worst of it was, I was most dead too. I got some mud and plastered over my head and back, and laid down along'side of that bar and stayed there all night and the next day. Then I got up and started for camp; but the boys thought I had gone along ahead, and they'd broke camp and left. So I had nothin' to do but to tramp all the way to the Post, forty miles or more, where I found the doctor who fixed me up as well as he could. I fetched the piece of scalp the bar took off along with me, but the doctor said it had got dried up, so it wan't no good to put on agin."

This was a thrilling bear-story; but I listened to one a few weeks before from a German at Lake Tahoe that promised a more tragic dénouement. "It was yoost a year ago last vinter," said Hans, "ven I vas comin' home from cuttin' wood mit mine axe on one sholer and mine rifle on the oder. I vasn't thinkin' of notin' but mine supper, ven yoost as I vas comin' down a hill vere dere vas big hole in the side, I sees big grizzly richt front of the hole. I never vas so froyht! Mine knees vas shake and mine hair vas stand straight. I vas tremble all over. But I says to mineself, 'Hans,' says I, 'that bear kill you or you kill the bear.' I know if I miss him I coont run for tree, because there wunt no tree there. So I steadied mineself little, and then I vant to make sure. So I crawls up to get round sage-brush so notings come in the vay. I takes up mine rifle, and yoost as I vas

goin' to fire, I looks again, and—it vas tam log!'"
Evidently it was no log that scalped Jeff.

Our road had been for the first part of the afternoon
mostly on level ground, but we now reached a district
of broken ridges. Passing over one of these elevations, my companion pointed out on our left a narrow
valley, through which ran a sluggish stream among
the thick willow-brush.

"That is a place," said he, "I shall never forget;
for there it was we fit the Injuns in the biggest kind
of a fight.   They ambushed us in them willows.
Every shot of them told on some of us, and we
couldn't git at 'em, they was stowed away so close in
the brush.   We lost twenty men, but we finally
drove 'em.   I tell you 'twas worse than fighting with
bars!

"Jest as the scrimmage was about over, poor Gus
Mellish was shot down close by me. I knowed Gus
well.   We'd been pardners in Californy.   He was one
of the best fellers I ever knowed, and we wus always
gettin' sells on one another.   But Gus got the heaviest thing on me when he died!

"As soon as he was shot, I see he was a goner. I
helped him up on the bank, and eased him off all I
could, sayin' over all the Bible I knowed, and pro-
misin' to give his watch and his gun to his folks.
But Gus wanted me to agree to send him to Frisco,

where his folks lived. So I promised, and he died happy.

"Well, I buried him on the spot temporary. Three years after, when I cal'lated he was about eat up, I went for his bones. Now what do you think Gus had been and gone and done? Why, as he was buried in alkali, he'd gone and turned himself into solid stone, and then he expected me to pay freight on him all the way to Frisco! I did it, though, but that was the last load Gus ever got on me!" When Jeff had concluded this touching reminiscence of his departed friend, he stopped his horse and took a drink to his memory.

At five o'clock we reached the little settlement of Weston, having, like all the others, its presiding bishop. Jeff had some accounts to settle with Bishop Moone. This prelate has only one wife, and consequently his family is not so large as that of Mr. Robbins. A pretty girl of sixteen gracefully offered us goblets of cream, and then we moved along.

Ten miles beyond was the village of Clarkson, where Jeff proposed to spend the night, as by the time we should arrive there our horses would have accomplished more than fifty miles on that day; and this, considering their heavy pack, would be enough for them. As for ourselves, the air was so exhilarating that we could easily have ridden on to Corinne, thirty-five miles farther.

Just before arriving at Clarkson we passed an ox-wagon. "How are you, Bishop?" exclaimed Jeff to the man driving the team; "we are going to quarter on you to-night." "All right, Jeff," said the Bishop, "ride on, and tell my folks to get supper, and not wait for me." We arrived at Clarkson at seven o'clock. One Mrs. Smith and the other Mrs. Smith received us very pleasantly, and set about the preparation ordered by the head that belongs to them both.

The Bishop arrived in time to say grace over some good milk, bread, butter, and stewed gooseberries, all of which were very appetizing. Our horses were turned out in the corral with plenty of oats and hay before them, and in the evening I played on a tin whistle and told stories to the young Mormon Smiths. A "brother" came in and informed the Bishop that there was to be "a special meeting of the greatest importance;" so he was obliged to bid us good-night.

As we proposed to leave at an early hour, I wished to settle our little bill, but neither the Bishop nor the Bishopesses would hear of it. They made us a bed on the floor, into which Jeff and I turned together, and then all was still in the Episcopal domain for the night, with the exception of occasional squalls from different babies in different corners of the log-cabin.

Bright and early we arose from our literally down bed of straw, caught our horses, saddled and packed, and were off and away before five o'clock. We passed through another settlement an hour afterwards. The Bishop of that diocese was just coming out, economizing time by buttoning his suspenders on his way to his daily labor.

"That Bishop Littlewood," said Jeff, "has got four wives, and as many children as you see chickens running 'round here; how he packs them all in that house"—it was a small, one-story log-cabin—"is what I can't understand myself. I would try to go in and see how he fixes things some time, if I thought there was room to get inside the door amongst the crowd."

After passing this little village, the Bear River takes a sudden turn from Cache Valley to the right, and makes its way through a deep cañon, the sides of which are so precipitous and rocky that there is no room for a road by the border of the stream. I was especially sorry for this, as we were obliged to make a détour, and that prevented us from seeing the cataract we could hear leaping and roaring through the chasm.

Below the cascade is an immense alkaline plain of more than two hundred thousand acres. It is now valueless, for no one cares to pre-empt a homestead or to buy of the government one hundred and sixty acres of such land, even at the price of one dollar and a quarter per acre—all that one individual can purchase. But if the government would sell the whole to a company, one would be speedily organized to take it ; and diverting Bear River from its channel above the falls, this great desert could all be irrigated, and would speedily increase fifty times in value by being able to produce forty or fifty bushels of wheat to the acre. The whole expense attending such an operation has been estimated to be less than one hundred thousand dollars. It is a magnificent scheme, and to accomplish it there is only required a judicious outlay of money at Washington, "where it will do the most good."

As we descended into the valley through which the river glides down to Corinne on its course into Great Salt Lake, the sun threw our long shadows over the plain, making us like very important coming events. It now began to grow quite warm, even before we reached the Montana stage-station at seven o'clock for breakfast. This is a small frame building belonging to the company, and is the first house not built of logs that I had seen for a long time.

After feeding ourselves and our animals, we galloped on rapidly in order to arrive before the intense heat of the day should overpower us, and soon saw the City of Corinne starting up on the plain, and resembling Cuxhaven as it is made from the North Sea

OUR ARRIVAL AT CORINNE.

It was nearly ten o'clock when we reached the town
and rode at once to the photograph saloon, where the
artist speedily made a picture of Jeff and myself as
we arrived from Cariboo. This performance having
been accomplished, we rode over to the " Bear River
Hotel," sent our horses out into the herd, washed,
dressed, shaved, dined, and rested for the remainder
of the day.

CHAPTER VIII.

THE city of Corinne is a village of some three hundred and fifty men—perhaps one thousand people, including women and children. It was founded from motives partly mercenary, partly religious and moral. It is twenty-four miles west of Ogden, the junction of the Central and Union Pacific Railroads, and is the nearest available point to Montana.

That great mining district receives its principal supplies from Corinne, from whence also there is daily stage communication over a route of five hundred miles through sage-brush deserts, steep cañons, and over bare mountains. It is a pleasant drive for those who like these things seasoned with plenty of dust. The freighting business is very brisk.

On the latter part of our route touching upon the Montana trail, we met and passed dozens of mule caravans going and returning. This trade, now being transferred to the Utah Northern Railroad, will continue until the completion of the Northern Pacific Railroad. When, if ever, that is accomplished, the people of Montana will dispense with Corinne, and its value as a trading mart will fall to zero.

Saints combined with sinners in the endeavor to build up Corinne—not "Latter-Day Saints," but all other kinds of saints who regard Mormonism as the abomination of desolation, Anti-Christ, the scarlet woman, and the beast of the Apocalypse.

They meant to plant a Christian landmark in its midst; to set up a bright and shining light that should throw its pure rays far and wide to scatter the darkness in which the "twin relic of barbarism" had shrouded the land. For this purpose churches and grog-shops were to act in harmony. Therefore there had been opened three of the former and twenty of the latter. The churches are supported by home missionary societies; the grog-shops are maintained by the voluntary system.

It was a sultry Sunday morning, and, after having slept and breakfasted at the shanty styled the "Bear River Hotel," I strayed about the town. My friend Jeff had introduced me to most of the three hundred and fifty resident gentlemen, and so I received nearly that number of invitations to take a drink, all of which were respectfully declined on the temperance stand-point. That is the only safe support to fall back upon with these hospitable gentlemen.

It was an unusually lively day. A great many teams happened to be in town, and the drivers and traders made the holiday uproarious. The order of exercises alternated with swearing and drinking all day long, and the evening must have been something fearful, for then the dance-houses would be in active operation.

Soon after eleven o'clock I made my way to the nearest church. I was told that it was Presbyterian. On approaching I heard the music of a psalm-tune, from which I inferred that the services had already commenced. On entering, however, I found the solitary musician seated at one of those sewing-machine "melodeons," and grinding out the Missionary Hymn.

He stopped on noticing the unexpected addition to the congregation, and entered into conversation. "There would be no meeting to-day." "In fact," he added, "we don't have any stated preaching; we have to get along as well as we can with what we pick up." In answer to further inquiries, he said that there were three societies, which he thus enumerated on the rising scale: "The Episcopal, they have one member to their church; the Methodist,

they have two ; but we have eleven communicants."
There was no little pride in the emphasis given to the
preponderance of Presbyterianism.

I ventured to make two suggestions for the better
maintenance of religious worship. One was that the
fourteen church-members should club together, and,
with the assistance of moral sinners outside the pale
of the church and the different home-missionary
societies, support one good minister in one meeting-
house, and rent out the other two to help pay expenses. " Why not ? "

" That wouldn't do," he said ; " we couldn't agree
on doctrine nor form." " Well, then," I proposed,
" get some minister more liberal than you are, who
for the sake of spreading the gospel would be willing
to be like St. Paul, ' all things to all men '—an Episcopalian one Sunday, a Methodist the next, and a
Presbyterian on a third. How would that do ? "
" Oh, pshaw ! " replied the organist, " such a fellow
would be a —— hypocrite."

So I shook off the dust from my shoes, and would
gladly have shaken off the dust from my clothes, and
left Corinne. I bade a warm adieu to my friend Jeff,
whose services as a guide up through Montana to
the Yellowstone Park I had partially engaged for the
next season, when, with tent-equipages, mules, and
horses, I propose, with such ladies and gentlemen

as fancy the enjoyments of fine air, mountain scenery, fishing, shooting, and camping out, to make a summer excursion.*

This Sunday was a blazing hot day at Corinne, in very unpleasant contrast to the weather experienced at Soda Springs and Cariboo. I waited till four of the afternoon, in the vain hope that the mercury would fall below ninety degrees, and then started on my pony for Ogden, a distance of thirty miles by the travelled road. For most of the route this lies north of the railway under the base of the mountains, and passes through several thriving Mormon settlements. The chief one is Brigham City, five miles east of Corinne. In all these towns the streets are wide, and shaded by lime or locust trees, streams of water from the public irrigating ditch running by the sidewalks on each side. All the house-lots, like those of Salt Lake City, are supposed to contain one and a

---

* Since writing this, I have received the following from Cariboo : "Your friend, Jeff Davis, was murdered here on Thursday, the 18th instant, by Jim Waters. We shall hang Jim, of course, for it was a clean, clear case of murder. We are only waiting for Perkins to get his liquor-bill settled up first. Jeff was sitting in the saloon, with his feet cocked up on a chair ; Waters came in, and without a word walked up and stabbed him twice near the heart. Jeff died in about seven hours, and has been decently buried at Soda Springs. I was not present when the unpleasantness occurred, or there might have been further interesting particulars." Alas, poor Jeff !

quarter acres of land each, which is invariably taste-
fully laid out as a garden ; thus, though the houses are
often poor and only of logs, they have an air of comfort
and beauty which is lacking in many more pretending
edifices.

In strange contrast to Corinne, here reigned the
peaceful quiet of the Sabbath day. Among its two
thousand inhabitants there is not one grog-shop or
disreputable house. Alas, how little has been the influence of the missionary city of Corinne on the be-
nighted people of Brigham City !

They were on their way to worship in their large
and very pretty " temple," most of them on foot, but
many coming from a distance in wagons—all decently
but not luxuriously dressed, the faces of the men sun-
burnt, but not whiskey-fired, and those of the women
certainly wearing no appearance of slavery or discon-
tent. Many of the young girls and children were
uncommonly pretty. Had I not been pressed for
time, and had not my travelling costume been so out
of place among the well-dressed crowd, I should certainly have stopped to worship with them, and should
doubtless have been as much edified as I was in
conversing with the organist in the conventicle at
Corinne.

I rode on, the sun pouring downwards and upwards too, with remorseless fierceness. There was

not a breath of air, and the reflection from the glassy
surface of the Salt Lake on my right and from the
heated rocks of the mountains on my left, made the
next hour almost insupportable for rider and horse.

Soon after six the air cooled somewhat, and a
breeze from the south came over the waters of the
lake, and brought a salty smell like the sea-breeze of
the ocean.

Elder Geo. Q. Cannon, now the delegate to Washington, and a man of sterling worth and talent, had
been preaching at Ogden, and I met several wagon-
loads of men, women, and children on their return. I
stopped at the door of a house just as the owner arrived. He was quite delighted with the Elder's sermon, and was generally jubilant on the subject of religion, which he exemplified by urging me to spend
the night, and on my declining to do so, in presenting
me with a tumbler of rich cream, in which offer there
was a more acceptable act of Christianity than in a
simple "cup of cold water."

Eight miles west of Ogden are some hot salt
springs, coming from a rock near the road, and forming quite a large basin of water. Dick, the pony,
here amused me by his astonishment. The little
rascal was always as "dry" as a Corinne Christian
and always making excuses to stop and take a drink.
When he came in sight of this clear-looking pool he

went for it incontinently, and when his forelegs were immersed to the knees by the jump which he made into the hot water, he gave a sudden squeal of pain, and executed a pirouette which would have unseated me if I had not anticipated it. It was curious to notice how daintily he approached the next stream crossing the road.

The railroad-traveller gets a very wrong impression of Ogden. .He sees nothing but the Gentile part of the town, the stations of the U. P. and C. P. Railroads, their offices and engine-houses, and a dozen or two shanties occupied as restaurants, grog-shops, and gambling-houses. The " city " is a mile above, under the base of the range of mountains, watered, as all the country is watered between it and Corinne, by mountain streams diverted from their courses by canals. I have already described Salt Lake City and Brigham City ; all Mormon towns are alike excepting in size, and of course in the style of architecture, which varies according to the time of settlement ; the more remote consisting exclusively of log-cabins. Salt Lake City, and those in its neighborhood, have substantial frame and brick buildings.

Ogden is a pretty and quiet town, somewhat larger than Brigham City. It was late when I arrived and found comfortable quarters at the Ogden Hotel.

At five o'clock punctually, on Monday morning,

little Dick stood saddled at the door of the hotel, and
we proceeded on our journey to Salt Lake City. In
this country people sleep out of doors when they can,
within their houses if they must. As I passed
through the village, I noticed that all the piazzas and
stoops had their sleeping occupants, and in some
cases they lay about on the ground. It is fortunate
that the climate thus allows a part of the inconvenience of a large family to be overcome.

The people were soon astir and the cows were
being driven from their corrals after milking. In the
daytime they are generally herded, the people of each
settlement contributing to pay a man to collect them
all, drive them to the plains outside, and return them
at evening. The animals become so accustomed to
their daily routine that on the sound of the horn they
form into line, and go out and come home with very
little trouble to the herdsman.

A young milkmaid filled my tin cup with fresh
morning milk, a better "eye-opener" than any tonic
bitters, and then I went on my way to the outskirts
of the settlement. There I was led astray by the
ignorance of a stupid son of one father and many
mothers, who told me to keep to the right when out
on the prairie. I did so, and after plodding along
through the sage-brush for two or three miles, found
that the trail led to the borders of the lake. So, re-

A PLEASANT BREAKFAST.

tracing my steps, I got back to the wagon-road with no pleasant feelings towards the youngster who had lengthened my journey at least five miles on this hot day.

Sixteen miles from Ogden is the little village of Kaysville. Twenty-one miles it was for Dick and me. Selecting the most attractive house, near which a farmer with six or eight stalwart sons was threshing out his wheat, I approached and asked if my horse could be fed.

" Of course he can," said Mr. Enhart, " and don't you want something to eat, too ? " Most certainly he surmised the truth. So one of the young men took charge of Dick, and I walked into the house, which more resembled a Hollander's cottage for scrupulous cleanliness than anything I ever saw in our country.

There were two matrons, evidently sisters, and two younger ladies, all about their household duties. There were children belonging to them collectively, besides the great lads outside, girls of sixteen to twenty years and young ones of a more tender age, and babies of scarcely any age at all. A bountiful repast of bread and butter, milk and honey, was spread before me, and while I sat at the table two gentle young Mormonesses kept the flies away, gracefully moving green switches over my head. What captivating addenda to a breakfast !

I have noticed these peculiarities in all Mormon families : the young people never speak unless spoken to, in presence of their elders, and when address-ing one wife, I always got replies from all, or as many of them as were present. And they all, too, seemed to possess the faculty of propounding to me the same question at the same time. I spoke in terms of admiration of the house and garden. "Yes," they all replied, "Mr. Enhart has a nice place." They seemed to think all things, including themselves, were Mr. Enhart's ; they had no possessive right in anything but in children, and those were "ours."

Babies are the great delight, and to bear them is the great ambition of Mormon women. Child-mur-der, the barbarous custom of civilized life, practised to an almost incredible extent in our large cities, where it is found "too expensive to have a family," cannot at any rate be laid to the charge of the "twin relic of barbarism" in Utah.

Here, at least among the country people, it is econ-omy to have a large family. They all work ; the little busy bee is not more active than a Mormon child. One of the Mrs. Enharts showed me a very neatly-sewed patchwork quilt made by "Vinny" at the age of nine. "Yes," exclaimed another Mrs. En hart, "my Josie made one of them when she was only seven !" I did not like to inquire how many children

each lady had, lest I might wound the feelings of
some wife less fortunate than the others. But the
children were all general stock—they were all " ours "
—the only articles of property, and those of priceless
value, which were not exclusively Mr. Enhart's.

After breakfast I strolled in the garden, where two
of the young Hebes were picking gooseberries. So
I picked gooseberries; and when I talked with one
young lady they both answered, as their mothers did,
and they both asked me the same questions simul-
taneously. They knew little of the outside world,
nor did they care to know. They were happy in
their ignorance of it.

The garden—I could not help thinking of the
garden of Eden, only there were two Eves instead of
one in it—was an acre in extent, and was full of most
delicious fruit : gooseberries, currants, blackberries,
apricots, pears, apples, peaches, and grapes, all but
the latter quite ripe, and of larger size and more
abundant on the trees and vines than we ever have
them at home. These women " tempted me, and I
did eat," and the good Lord did not take offence ; at
any rate, He did not send any angel with a two-edged
sword after us.

The eldest Mrs. Enhart gave me a most interesting
account of their early experiences in Utah. She was
in the first band that came after the pioneers. The

story of the Plymouth pilgrims is not more replete
with the memories of hardship and danger. What a
long tramp those zealous Mormons had over a trackless
desert, sterile plains, and rocky mountains worse to
endure, surrounded as they were not only by natural
obstacles, but by mortal foes, a thousand times worse
than the Atlantic storms that beat upon the " May-
flower ! "

Like those old pilgrims, they were sustained by a
great idea. They lived on that idea, and they were
willing to die for it. In neither case was it " for the
right of every man to worship God according to the
dictates of his own conscience." That would have
been a nobler cause than ever was maintained by
either Puritan or Mormon. They both fled from
religious persecution, to find a land which they might
appropriate to themselves for their own system of
worship, and for that alone.

Exactly parallel have been the cases thus far, and
parallel they will continue. When the Quakers and
the Baptists endeavored to maintain their religious
tenets among the Puritans, they were told to " go
away from their midst," and if they refused to go
they were persecuted. By-and-by New England
became settled by all denominations in spite of
intolerant edicts, and now bigotry has no power.

Precisely in this spirit did the Mormons endeavor

to warn off the Gentiles who came to Utah. They refused to leave. Then they persecuted them, as they themselves had been persecuted. But that great missionary, the Union Pacific Railroad, came along step by step, and when the last rail was spiked in Utah, universal toleration echoed to the sound of the hammer ; and now all past bickerings and persecutions should be forgotten, and different Christianities and civilizations allowed to work themselves out side by side.

Mrs. Enhart said, that as they toiled along the road they all supposed that as soon as they arrived they would find rich prairies and green meadows— everything ready to plant their seed and to commence raising their herds.

" And lucky it was we did not know what was before us," she added, " for when we got through Emigration Cañon and saw nothing but sage-brush, sand, and alkali, if we had not had faith we should have died. But Brother Brigham told us it was all right—this was the place. It was a desert, but God would make it ' blossom as the rose ; ' and thanks be to Him, He has. He has blessed us as he never blessed any people before !

"Anyway, I am happy, when I think what we have been through. The first year we planted our seed, nothing came of it ; the second, the crickets destroyed everything; then came the grasshopper plague. In that year, in one day, our boys shoveled them into sacks and buried over fifty bushels of them in a hole. The air was full of the horrid smell of the dead insects, and we all feared a plague in addition to the loss of the crop. But look at things now. Wasn't President Young right? We have always found his advice right, because he has revelations from God, and what you see all round here proves it."

Far was it from me to dispute with the good lady, or to attempt to weaken her faith in the divine mission of Brigham Young, because she could not disconnect it from faith in God. I thanked her for her story, and thanked them all, old and young, for their kindness and hospitality; and Dick then jogged along with his paunch filled with oats, and I had as many apricots and gooseberries as my pockets would hold.

For the remainder of the way to Salt Lake City, a distance of twenty-five miles, there is an almost constant succession of little hamlets and single farmhouses, surrounded by gardens, and often with shade-trees planted upon the street. On this hot day a few more of them would have made me grateful, but as they, like all other green things here, require irrigation, they are only seen in the neighborhood of dwellings.

At noon I reached Sessions, a large town distant

ten miles from Salt Lake City. Resting here awhile, and having dined at the hotel, I attained my destination early in the afternoon, having accomplished eighty miles in the last twenty-four hours. The whole ride from Cariboo is two hundred and fifty miles, and the time occupied on the road was five days.

It had been a delightful journey, and it gave me an insight of the domestic life and character of the people not easily attained by any other mode of travel, besides affording the best opportunities of viewing the fine scenery and estimating the agricultural value of the land.

CHAPTER IX.

LITTLE Cottonwood Cañon is the location of the principal silver mines of Utah. They are by no means, however, confined to it, but are to be found in almost every mountain of the Wasatch and Western ranges which enclose the Salt Lake Valley.

The easiest way to approach this district is by the Utah Southern Railroad, as far as Sandy, and then by the narrow-gauge railroad, a marvel of engineering skill, to Granite City, its present terminus. This little road has overcome a grade of two hundred feet to the mile, and if it is continued to Alta, the head of the cañon, the ascent will be much greater and seemingly impossible. The whole distance of rail to Granite City from Salt Lake City is eighteen miles, and thence the trip is generally made on horseback, over a very rough wagon-freight road of ten miles.

Being still the owner of little Dick, and having a greater liking at all times for the comfortable Mexican saddle and the fresh air than for a railroad-car with its atmosphere of many breaths, I found it more agreeable to accomplish the whole distance of twenty-eight miles on horseback.

I left the town at an early hour on Sunday, August 24th, before many people were astir. The shadows of the eastern mountains, beneath which was my path, were thrown over the road, while the western range was glowing in the sunlight, gradually extending into the valley at their base, until suddenly, as I passed the mouth of Emigration Cañon, the dazzling sun-blaze broke through it upon the whole plain.

I had promised to breakfast with an "apostate" gentleman, who lived five miles from the city. Before describing my arrival at his comfortable farm-house, I will state, from the most reliable authority, that in the city of Salt Lake the Gentile population may be considered one-sixth, and in the territory generally, one-tenth of the whole. Besides the Mormons and the Gentiles, there is at present a small but rapidly increasing percentage of apostates—people who have been Mormons, but are Mormons no longer. My friend Simmons is one of these.

An apostate is a man who asserts that he has seen the error of his ways, and has accordingly re-

nounced the Mormon faith.   Sometimes you will find
them sincere, sometimes not.

I find it hard to believe that, in this age of the
world, any educated man can have, or have had, a real
faith in the inspiration of Joe Smith or of Brigham
Young, while I am not surprised that those who were
taught it in their infancy should remain conscientious
believers.   It is no more strange that they should
implicitly credit the story of Joe Smith's receiving
heavenly revelations on golden plates than it is that
we should believe that Moses talked with God and
received the divine commandments on stone tablets.
I apprehend that most people believe in their
various religions because they were taught them by
their parents, and I do not know why young Mormons should be exceptions.   But I do not understand
how a man of fair education can embrace Mormonism
de novo with sincerity.

Therefore it is that the apostates here are not generally the young men and women, but they are found
among those who originally "came out from the
world."   It is not fair to say that every educated
person who thus joined the church was a hypocrite,
nor that every uneducated person who joined it was a
fool.   Nevertheless, it is true that most of the hypo-
crites are among the former class, and most of the
fools are among the latter.   There are apostates from

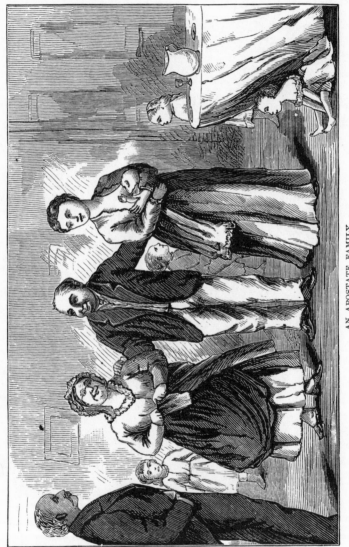

AN APOSTATE FAMILY.

both these divisions : from the first, because they find
that the religion no longer "pays ;" and from the last,
because they become educated by association with
Gentiles, and are really convinced of their error.

Besides the out-and-out apostates there are secta-
rians, such as the Godbeites and the Morrisites, who
accept most of the Mormon faith, ruling out the
practice of polygamy ; but these are few in number.

Among the apostates polygamy is of course supposed to be at once discarded, and so when I rode up
to my friend Simmons's door, I anticipated the welcome of a quiet little Gentile Christian family.   What
was my surprise, then, at beholding a perfect bee-
hive !

I was first introduced to Mrs. S. No. 1, and then to
Mrs. S. No. 3, the intermediate lady having been
lost to the family a year or two since.   Then there
were a number of boys and girls approaching the
innumerable.   Mr. S., who takes count of them occasionally, said the last census gave eleven boys and
twelve girls.

"Good gracious, Simmons !" I exclaimed, "I
thought you had been an apostate for sixteen years.
Whose little four-year-old is this ? " " Why, he's mine,
of course," he replied, " and that's his mother," pointing to a comely, smiling young woman who stood lean-
ing affectionately on the shoulder of the elder Mrs. S.

"You see how it was," continued the head of the family; "when I apostatized I had three wives. What was I going to do ? Were we going to turn two of 'em adrift on the cold charity of the world ? Could we do that, my dear ?" The elder Mrs. S., who was thus appealed to, said, "Certainly not," and the younger Mrs. S. just had the merriest twinkle in her eye, and they all laughed, and I laughed too. "Well, of course," continued Mr. S., "we all had to live together—and more children would come." "Naturally," I observed. "Yes, naturally," echoed my host, "we could not help that, you know." Well, as Mr. Simmons was contented, and the two Mrs. S. were contented, and the twenty-three children were contented, I did not think their little family arrangement was any business of mine. Simmons did not say so, but his circumstances and surroundings clearly evinced that, so far from considering polygamy as the damning spot in the texture of his former religion, he thought it the only piece of the whole cloth worth saving.

After breakfast I pursued my way for a short distance on the plain, which is everywhere well cultivated, and then mounted a few feet on to the level "bench" where the land is principally used for pasture.

The great Salt Lake Valley, besides enclosing the lake itself, a sheet of water ninety miles long by forty wide, consists of low levels for fifty miles north and south, bordered on the east by the Wasatch range of mountains, whither I was bound, and on the west by the Oquirrh range.

Both ranges are intersected by various cañons or valleys of sharp descent, whence the mountain-streams pour with great velocity and abundance into the River Jordan, which, taking its rise at the southern limit of the valley in a fresh-water lake, terminates in the great Salt Lake at the north.

All along the foot-hills, at various elevations from the plain, are clearly defined terraces, called "benches," that were at different epochs the shores of an immense lake which gradually dwindled down from its highest elevation to its present level, and in the course of ages, as is evident from the landmarks of even the last thirty years, will disappear altogether.

Cache Valley and the other valleys of the north, through which I have recently travelled, have precisely the same formation. Every one of them, like this of Salt Lake, when left by the waters, became an alkaline desert. Every one of them, like this, if the same simple system of irrigation is pursued, may become a garden.

All that is done here is to dig wide and deep ditches across the mouths of the streams at the various foot-hills from north to south, from which the water is let off at convenient distances by sluices into the low grounds.

It matters not to this people if no drop of rain falls in the summer. Plenty of snow falls on the mountains in the winter; some of it yet remains there, though it gradually melts and runs off in copious streams. The old alkali of the plains, saturated by the artificial overplus of the waters, becomes a fertilizer. No manure is or will be required. Thirty, forty, sometimes fifty, and occasionally seventy bushels of wheat are produced to the acre by this cheap process of agriculture.

Now, as I ride along the bench, what a different view is on either side! how sharply does this bench divide the grand and the beautiful! Towering snow-clad cliffs two thousand feet above me, on the left; thousands of acres of grain-covered and garden-spotted plains just below on my right; and thus I go on till the cañon of Big Cottonwood opens most grandly.

But there is not my road. A mile or two beyond —for the ridge between them, though two thousand feet high, comes to a sharp dividing point—I enter what is called "Little Cottonwood Cañon," although it is by far the deeper cut of the two. Its littleness of width is its beauty, for it is so narrow that the cliffs

52265

on either side are almost perpendicular. In the hollow a wide, rushing stream thunders noisily along, always on the descent, and sometimes leaping in steep cascades. By its side is the wagon-road and the narrow-gauge railroad, over which a train of cars was slowly struggling up the hill.

We arrived together at Granite City. This city owes its present importance to the fact that here the railroad terminates just now, and the wagon-traffic begins. When the road is completed farther up, Granite City will move up too. This will be easily effected by drinking all the whiskey in it and pulling down the houses and putting them up again, and re-stocking them with whiskey. The whole process of changing the base of this city can be effected in two days.

The remaining ten miles to Alta City is often difficult to accomplish on account of the vast number of loaded teams descending with ore from the upper mines. This is brought by wagons, in strong bags, containing each eighty to one hundred pounds, and being transferred to the railroad at Granite City, is carried to the smelting-works in the valley.

The passenger-train had just discharged its travellers, who here procured horses, and I thus found myself in a large company. It was lively work, dodging the descending teams and passing slow horsemen;

and all this travel raised a cloud of dust so blinding that there was some little danger of pitching headlong into the torrent below. Occasionally the dusty cloud would clear up, and then we had magnificent views all around us, while almost constantly at our sides were those perpendicular granite walls. As we progressed, the mountains were found well timbered. It was curious to be able to estimate the depth of the snow in winter, for in that leisure season most of the wood-felling is done. The stumps were mostly from ten to twelve feet high, that being the level of the snow from which the trees were cut.

Four or five miles above Granite City, and about the same distance from Alta, the marks of the great avalanche of last winter were pointed out to us. Seven men with twelve mules were drawing ore on sleds, when suddenly an immense body of snow, a quarter of a mile in extent, came down from the mountain on our left from a height of fifteen hundred feet, crushing trees and boulders of rock on its way, and sweeping along far across the river the unfortunate teamsters and all the mules but one, which in some way made its escape. For all the rest of the winter, the spring, and most of the summer, they lay buried in the snow, and but recently were discovered, stiffly frozen in their icy shrouds. Long will the spot be remembered, and many an anxious glance will be cast aloft as men in winter pass hurriedly along this part of the trail.

At noon we arrived at Alta City, the head of the cañon, and situated directly under the celebrated Emma Mine.

CHAPTER X.

I HAD scarcely deposited my cantinas on the stoop of the hotel, when I was approached by at least a dozen mining speculators or brokers with offers of "valuable prospects" and "richly developed mines." Let me here explain that "prospects" are small excavations, not much larger than badger-holes, in the sides of the mountains. There are tens of thousands of them in this and other cañons. The hills are honeycombed with them. "Richly developed mines" are likewise plentiful, but most of the riches are put in, and too often little in return is taken out. Now and then, as in the case of the "Emma," the "Flagstaff," and some few others, more is taken out than is put in. But it is doubtful if the English capitalists who buried five million pounds sterling in the Emma will be able to dig one million of it out. I secured a seat at the table as far as possible from the crowd that had assaulted me, so that I might peacefully enjoy my dinner, which was a very good one ; and it may be added that Mr. Fuller's hotel is in all respects a remarkably excellent house, considering its locality.

In the afternoon I made the acquaintance of Mr. Thomas Sweeney, who assured me that the New York Alderman of the same name was no relative of his. So I trusted more readily to his guidance and information.   We first walked up to the Emma Mine.

"Now," says Mr. Sweeney, "I'll tell you what, there's some queer capers going on, as there have always been going on, about that Emma." Thereupon he went back into its early history, and from his statements, corroborated by those of others, this is it : The actual discovery of the mine, like that of great continents and inventions, is somewhat involved in obscurity.   A certain Mr. Smith first stumbled on it, but Mr. Woodman, whom I afterwards met, assured me that he made the first practical exploration in the year 1865.   In 1868 Mr. Woodman and his partner offered one-quarter of the mine for $3,000, and could not find a purchaser.   They had then worked down eighty-five feet, and commenced shipping and selling their ore.   Before that, they were so reduced that in their log-cabin they actually suffered for want of food.

After they had proved the value of the mine to

5*

some extent, Walker Brothers, of Salt Lake, paid them $25,000 for one-sixth, and then Mr. Hussey paid them $25,000 for one-quarter of it.   These parties thereupon altogether sold the whole to Parks and Baxter for $750,000, which large sum these gentlemen actually realized from the products of the mine.

Then came in a great deal of dark financial management, in which Mr. Sam Ten Eyck, whom I saw at Parley Park where he is now operating on a new mining scheme, claims to have borne a conspicuous part. Senator Stewart, of Nevada, in some way or other, is said to have made $100,000 out of these manœuvres. Whether Mr. Schenck, our Minister to London, made any money or not is not positively known, but that he lost a great deal of reputation is notorious.   Finally, through the instrumentality, direct or indirect, of all these parties, the Emma Mine was "stocked" in the English market for £1,000,000, in 50,000 shares of £20 each.   The mine had paid for itself to its previous owners.   This immense sum was all clear profit, less undiscovered brokers' commissions.

Eighteen per cent. dividend was guaranteed to the stockholders for the first year—nothing was said about the second year ; but poor gullible John Bull was led to suppose that the dividend would be yet more abundant.   The price of shares rushed rapidly up to £33. The eighteen per cent. was punctually paid out of the sale of ore which had been reserved for that purpose. The sellers could well have afforded to pay it even if none had been produced. In the second year the dividend was nothing. The stock fell to £2.10s., is now about £4, and what it will be in the future is a mystery.

There are two theories in Alta. One is that the vein has actually given out and the mine is worth nothing; the other is that there is a rich deposit in sight, capable of producing 100 tons per day, whereas the policy now is to turn out only fifteen tons, in order to "bear down" and buy in the stock. One supposition or the other is likely to be true, but I would not like to speculate on either.

It is some satisfaction that, whatever may have been the sharp practice of Americans in the first place, the present "devilish sly" trick and secrecy is being performed and maintained by Englishmen, who now control the affairs of the mine.

At the entrance of the shaft are various stagings, buildings, and offices connected with its operations. We applied to the proper person for liberty to enter the bowels of the precious earth, and met with a decided though courteous refusal. There were then evidently secrets down there, and secrecy was to be maintained for the speculative purposes already indicated. This stamps the present as well as the past management a swindle. The stock of the Emma Mine is on the open market, and if it is the desire of those who control it that the public should know its real value, there should be no concealment of this kind. Surely, then, be the mine valuable or valueless, it is a stock-jobbing fraud.

I was once refused admittance to a pin-factory in Birmingham, lest I should steal the trade, and now was refused admittance to a British mine, lest the public should know the value of their own property.

Some little statistical data were, however, afforded. The tunnel is 375 feet long ; the shaft, 400 feet deep ; 150 men are daily employed. The average value of the ore is from $150 to $200 per ton, 42 per cent. of which is lead, and 100 ounces of it to the ton is silver—and that is all that could be learned from the clerk of the office ; and so we descended to the hotel.

Seated around the bar-room stove—for it is always cold at night in Alta—I asked of several miners how many mines they supposed there might be within fifty miles of Salt Lake City.

"Well, in the first place," replied a pretty thorough ly informed man, "let me tell you the chief mining districts. These are : Little Cottonwood, Big Cotton-wood, American Fork, Parley Park, Argenta, Snake Creek, Bingham, Rush Valley, Dry Cañon, Ophir, Columbia, Lake Side, Tintic, Camp Floyd, North

Star, West Star, East Star, South Star, Mount Nebo, and several more."

Then my informant, with the interpolation of others, began to enumerate the best mines in these various districts, after this manner : " Emma, Vallejo, South Star, Flagstaff, Illinois Tunnel, Ohio, Savage, Gray Rock, Montezuma, Last Chance, Highland Chief, Reed & Benson, Monitor, Magnet, Titus, Western Star, Belle, Hiawatha, Lilliwah, Gophir, Revolution, Hidden Treasure, Crœsus, Pioneer, Idaho, McHenry, McKay, Home Ticket, Rockford, Emma Dagmar, Davenport, Mary, Excelsior, Amy May, Imperial Tunnel, White Cloud, Grizzly, Pocahontas, Baltic, Lavinia, Regulation, Darlington, City Rock, Cedar, Royal George, Roxford, Pleasant View, Fuller, Frederick, Enterprise, Superior, Buckeye, Golden Gate, Hershell, Gladiator, Wellington, Webster, Peruvian, Skipper, Oxford, Geneva, Clipper, Daisy, Jacob Astor, Ida, Emily, Louisa, Sedan, Lexington, Little Giant—" " Stop ! stop ! gentlemen," I exclaimed, " these surely cannot be all productive mines ? " " Oh yes they are, and there are lots more, to say nothing of prospects." In short, and not to weary the reader with more of this, these miners and others whom I met in other districts agreed on the average with this broad statement. There are around Salt Lake more than 30,000 locations, including working mines and prospects, of which over a thousand are in operation, employing more than twenty first-class and several small furnaces, and ten thousand men in operating the whole.

The value of production is over $6,000,000 annually. To whose benefit does this enormous wealth accrue? Not to the working miners, who are always "prospecting" and always poor, but to rich capitalists and thriving speculators. Doubtless the mountains are full of silver and lead, and if capital could be obtained to work all these thirty thousand prospects and a hundred thousand more which might be found, silver would so glut the world's markets that its purchasing value would be materially reduced. But only a few of the largest mines are worked to their full capacity, while most of even those are used simply for stock-jobbing purposes.

The proceedings cited in regard to the Emma apply to many of the rest. A mine is bought for a few thousand dollars, and by trickery or false representations is "put on the market" for hundreds of thousands or millions, which, if operated on the basis of its true value, would yield paying dividends. With the present fraudulent system it pays nothing to the deluded purchasers. But the mines will all contribute largely to the prosperity of Utah and especially to that of Salt Lake City, by bringing in population and

capital, and enhancing the value of real-estate. The
safest speculation is not in mines, but in houses and
lands.

On the next day, under the pilotage of Mr. Sweeney,
I climbed the hills, looked into a hundred small holes
or " prospects," talked with the miners, who in their
poverty were living on rich hopes for the future, and
then, my previous experience in gold mines at Cariboo
serving as a warning to be careful, prepared to leave
Little Cottonwood without yielding to the temptation
of silver.

CHAPTER XI.

OF Alta City itself there is little to be said. It is a small mining camp that is dignified by this high-sounding name, and a mining camp anywhere in this region is simply a collection of rough cabins and drinking " saloons."

A little half-finished shanty among the grog-shops and team-stables of Alta serves for a house of Methodist worship on Sundays, and for a court-house on days when justice is to be administered.

On Sunday evening, as is my wont among Mormons or Gentiles, I directed my steps to the house of worship. Alas for the Christianity of this mining camp ! All the denominations could number only two hearers thus far. The minister, who sat patiently behind the rough deal pulpit-stand, waiting for more to come, rose with a smile of satisfaction on his countenance when I entered, and shouted, " Welcome, my brother, you make three, and the Lord hath said that wherever two or three are gathered together in His name, He will be with them and bless them. I was going to start on two, but now I have got the full number, I feel still more encouraged."

So he started and bellowed as if he had been preaching in the open fields to an audience as numerous as one of those preached to by Wesley or Whitfield. One by one the congregation increased, each addition giving him encouragement to scream louder, until before the services closed the assembly amounted to eight and a half, including a woman and a nursing baby.

The cellar of the building is used as a prison, and a few gentlemen who were confined beneath for various infringements of the law, such as stealing, shooting, and stabbing, occasionally interrupted the exercises with their cat-calls and imprecations. These only caused our Boanerges to exert his lungs the more to overcome the disturbance.

There is a greater semblance of judicial form here than in some of the more distant camps and settlements. Where there is least of it there is really a greater security of property and life. Where a man can reasonably expect to hang on the nearest tree a few moments after discovery, he is not so apt to steal as he would be if his punishment were less ; and frequent as personal encounters are, murderers have not the encouraging hopes of Stokes, that trial after trial can be had, and that the chance of hanging is, after all, very remote.

Religion of any kind, I am sorry to say, is at a low ebb in Alta; while bar-rooms, faro-tables, and licentiousness are in the full tide of prosperity.

On the next day court was held in the same building. The judge, a miner clothed in imaginary ermine for the occasion, occupied the pulpit of yesterday, which was a literal bench then, and now besides it was a judicial one. The ermine was truly metaphorical, for he sat with no dress over his shirt-sleeves, cigar in mouth, his feet resting upon the desk. The lawyers, one of whom was a teamster and the other a miner, were in the same loose attire, and paid this deference to the Court, that they smoked pipes instead of Havanas.

The case was one of larceny. A Chinese cook of a restaurant had been accused by his employer of giving away provisions, notably cucumbers, to some of his countrymen outside. To every point of the direct examination of witnesses, the defendant's lawyer cried, "Your honor, I object." And to every item brought out by the cross-examination the plaintiff's lawyer shouted the same words.

The defence admitted that his client held the master's cucumbers in his hands, but his hands were

COURT AT ALTA CITY.

not out of the window when the cucumbers left them. "They were inside the window, and the outside Chinamen reached in and took them. Therefore they, if they could be found, should be declared guilty, not my client."

The plaintiff's counsel argued in this wise : "Was his hands clinched on the cowcumbers when t'other Chinamen come for 'em, or was they open? Why the —— didn't he hold on to 'em ? "

His Honor by this time had finished his cigar. Then he rose from the bench and commanded silence by striking his fist on the desk. "This here case is dismissed," he said. "It's too thin ; thinner'n ary slice of cowcumber ever I see. The time of the Court is too valooable to be took up with any such —— nonsense ! " So the Court, the lawyers, the plaintiff, and defendant all adjourned to the saloon where the larceny had been committed, and "took a drink all round."

On Tuesday afternoon, August 26, I mounted little Dick and wended my way up to the "divide" on the mountain-top which separates this cañon from the head of Big Cottonwood, passing Grizzly Flat, another mining camp, two miles above Alta.

After an ascent of two miles more, I reached the summit at an elevation of eleven thousand feet above the level of the sea, wading through the snow, and

facing a wind cold as a winter's blast.   But the air was
clear of clouds or mist, and the view down the two
cañons which lay before me was magnificent, totally
beyond my powers of description.

Crossing over, I began the steep descent, and came
into a thick and high forest of pines.   Following the
trail for an hour longer, I came down to a lovely
meadow, perched still high in the mountains by which
it was surrounded.   In its centre was a little clear,
transparent lake, and by its side the rude but taste-
fully built log-cabin of Mr. Brighton, a Mormon gentleman, who for health, and also for mining purposes,
makes this romantic spot his summer residence.

Here I received a cheerful welcome, and while I
dined from trout just caught from the lake, Dick was
turned loose to enjoy the feed on the broad lawn,
with the horses and cattle of my host.

" Aye, it is a sweet spot," said Mr. Brighton, as we
watched the sunset creeping of the high mountain
shadows over the plain ; " it 'minds me of my ain
hame in the Hielands."   And I, too, thought of many
a Highland hill and dale, seen long ago, though no
Scottish mountain or glen could equal the scene
before us.

Rising early in the morning after refreshing sleep,
and then enjoying a hearty breakfast, of which " oat-
meal parritch " formed a welcome part, I took leave

of my kind entertainer and his family, receiving his directions for Parley Park.

"Ye'll gang doon a mile or twa to the sa'-mill, and then ye'll tak the trail to the richt, and keep along till ye come to anither trail, a sma' bit awa' to the left, gin ye come to a bit wood, where ye gang to the richt, then to the left; then ye'll circle the mountain, and ye canna gang wrang." He added to these clear directions the information that "Kimball's," at Parley Park, lay at a distance of twelve miles.

CHAPTER XII.

I STARTED at 7 o'clock, and reached the saw-mill
without much difficulty, and there, of course, remembrance failed me. Out of all the trails that presented themselves, Dick was allowed to make a selection, and the result was that Dick and his rider were
lost in the wilds of the Wasatch Mountains.

All that I knew was that Parley Park bore about N.
W., and in so far as mountains, rocks, and precipices
allowed, I endeavored to steer that course, with the
sun for my guide. After wandering for four hours
in this way, I came upon a wagon-road, which trended
to a valley, and far in the distance below lay a town.
Descending towards it, totally uncertain of what it
might be, to my unutterable joy I at last met a man
on horseback.

" Where is Parley Park ? " I asked. " Parley Park !
Why, as near as may be, it is right over your horse's

tail!" "How far is it?" "Well, about twelve miles. Turn round, keep up the hill with me, and I will show you where to turn into the trail."

Guided by clearer directions than those of Mr. Brighton, I soon left my companion, and, crossing over Flagstaff peak, enjoyed such an extensive view of Provo Valley and Southern Utah, that I was not sorry for all my long deviation, as these are portions of the Territory which I did not subsequently visit.

I stood now like Moses on Mount Pisgah, satisfied, like him, to see the promised land, even if my foot should not press its soil. This journal would be more complete if it touched upon all points of Utah. Over the whole Territory, the mountains, cañons, and prairies are of the same character, and probably Provo, and other towns far away on the plain below me, are not unlike those I have already seen and propose yet to visit. I will forgive and even thank Mr. Brighton for having made me spend nearly a day on horseback to accomplish twelve miles, that I might see them in the distance.

Now keeping along on a well-defined trail, I reached the ranch of Mr. Snyder at two o'clock, and dined.

Snyder keeps a semi-hotel. He was away from home—from that home, I mean, for Snyder has three ranches and three families ; but the Mrs. Snyder of this ranch, who has half a dozen children—what the other Mrs. Snyders may have I do not know—provided me with an excellent dinner.

While I was at the table, Snyder came to this home, fresh from the visit of a week to another wife. At the sound of his horse's hoofs, up jumps the present Mrs. S., lays the baby in the cradle, cries, " Here comes father ! " and rushes out to fall upon his neck, and kisses him. Queer people, these Mormons !

After dinner I rode on six miles farther to Kimball's, passing on the way a summer encampment from Fort Douglas. Captain Ellis had pitched his tents in a romantic glen, and it was a pleasant sight to behold some ladies playing croquet on the green sward, the wagons drawn up in military order, the soldiers forming for evening parade, and the animals picketed on the rich grass.

Passing over the last divide, Parley Park lay beneath me. It is well named a park, for nature has done all its own work for it with that of art made to her hand.

It is like the plateau of Brighton's, only vastly enlarged. Mountains are all around a meadow-plain of five thousand acres of grass, through which a beautiful trout-stream meanders along. Fronting the centre of this level is the Kimball Hotel, the favorite summer retreat, as well it may be, of the people of Salt Lake, who have the leisure and the means to

spend a few days or weeks in this invigorating atmosphere of the hills.

The landlord of the hotel is a son of the late Heber
C. Kimball, whom Artemus Ward particularized as
"the most married man ᴧ Utah." His descendants
already number four hundred and forty-nine. His
son, "Bill," whom he christened William, after using
up all the Old Testament names, is more moderate
than his father in his conjugality, having only three
wives. As he resides two-thirds of the time at Parley
Park, and the other third of it at Salt Lake, he keeps
two wives here and one there.

The public are satisfied with this arrangement, for
the two ladies of this establishment are most excellent housekeepers and cooks, and this is what chiefly
concerns us. Cleaner linen can nowhere be found on
beds, and a better table was never spread; and all
this comfort and luxury is to be had for the very
moderate price of ten dollars per week. Mr. Kimball
is also a large farmer, and raises a great deal of other
stock besides the family kind.

Mormonism has great advantages for taking up
government land. No man can pre-empt more than
one hundred and sixty acres for himself; but each
child can do likewise, and thus the Kimball family, as
they increase, are becoming the owners of this rich
plain. By and by they will have two thousand head

of cattle, and will cut two thousand tons of hay, for which the City of Salt Lake will afford a ready market.

There is plenty of fishing and shooting in the neighborhood, although not so abundant as I found it at the north, the ground being more ranged by sportsmen. Still there was enough to afford ample occupation for the next two days for the little party of friends who joined us from town.

On Saturday I left this charming spot, and rode on for twenty-five miles to Salt Lake, avoiding the travelled and more level road, and passing down through Emigration Cañon, by which gate the first band of Mormon settlers, under the leadership of Brigham Young, entered upon their new home in 1847, after their long, tedious, patient journey of four months across the desert.

And now, twenty-six years later, I was riding over a good macadamized road, which led me out upon fruitful fields into the view of a large and thriving city, over the same route by which they arrived at these once barren plains.

As I turned around each succeeding rocky point, I could well imagine how it was gazed upon by them as they hoped it was the last, and when the last was actually reached and passed, and the full view of the valley burst upon my sight, the picture of that devoted band was as clearly present to me as if it had been depicted on canvas like that life-like painting of the Western emigrants that is seen in the Capitol at Washington. It seemed that as I listened I might yet catch the echo of their glad hosannas ringing through those Rocky Mountains safely passed at last!

I believe in the utter absurdity and imposture of the Mormon faith, so far as it differs from the recognized tenets of Christianity; but I believe in the sincerity of the great majority of its adherents, and I want no better proof of this than their history.

The persecutions endured by the Israelites at the hands of the Egyptians were as nothing in comparison with those suffered by the Mormon people at the hands of their nominally Christian countrymen, who drove them from one settlement and State to another, until they formed a resolution to put themselves, as they fondly hoped, forever beyond their reach.

Brigham Young, with all his prophetic instinct, never dreamed that they could be molested here. On his dreary journey, and shortly before his arrival, he was met by a Mormon missionary returning from California. He depicted in glowing colors the beauties of that region, its lovely climate, its fertile soil, its claim to be what it has since so amply proved, a second paradise. Brigham listened patiently to his report, and then replied, " All that shows that it is no place for us—the Gentiles would rout us out."

He had never yet seen the Salt Lake Valley, but he knew that it was a desert. He had an inspiration, however, which he chose to call a " revelation," that this was the destination of his people, and that the Almighty would change the desert to a garden for them.

It must be remembered, moreover, that at this time Utah was Mexican Territory. Once settled there, the Mormons would owe no allegiance to the United States government, and as to the Mexicans, they had no fear of them. In their eyes they were merely Canaanites, and " the sword of the Lord and of Gideon" would be the arbiter of any controversy with them that they might have.

The " revelation" given to Brigham Young designated the precise spot where the city of the New Jerusalem should be located. As they came out through Emigration Cañon, the little army of believers turned to the right, obedient to the direction of their leader, and marched four miles, before he cried " Halt!" Every individual came to a standstill. A fervent prayer of thanksgiving to Almighty God, their preserver, was offered, and ended with a loud and joyful " Amen!"

After this act of faith there followed immediately

one of the grandest acts of works on record, and these two great ideas of faith and works have been ever since the guiding stars of their eminently practical religion.

Before a moment's rest was allowed to man or beast, other than the time occupied by the prayer— before a mouthful of food could be eaten, the animals were unhitched from the wagons and yoked to the ploughs, the furrows were turned, an irrigating ditch was dug, the seed planted; and then they rested from their labors, and now their works do follow them.

History has no parallel to the energy and perseverance of this people. They were nurtured and made robust by the fillip of persecution, so that when they left the banks of the Missouri they were hardened to the work before them.

The journey of Moses and the Israelites, even with its pillar of fire before them, pales into insignificance compared with this. Let us accept our own revelation, while we ridicule that of the Mormons. Then we see God on the side of Israel, tormenting their persecutors with plague, pestilence, and famine ; opening seas and rivers for them that they might pass dry-shod ; making water to gush from the rock ; raining down vegetable and animal food ; helping them when they were too lazy to help themselves, and fighting their battles for them ; they all the time repining, growling, and apostatizing, and, after all, accomplishing in forty years what they should have done in a month.

Look now at these Latter-Day Saints!—not only at this company of pioneers, but at each succeeding host; more especially the hand-cart expedition of 1856, when six hundred men, women, and children started from Iowa, in July, dragging their babies, their property and provisions; crossing the Rocky Mountains in the snows of November; losing two hundred of their number on the road by death; yet never murmuring, but every morning and night thanking the Lord who had brought them thus far on their way.

Did not He know their sincerity, it must have sounded like irony in his ears! The " devil," we are told, " is good to his own." Surely, if these were his children, he showed his kindness strangely. Ah! they were no children of his; but they were fulfilling a mission of the same Almighty Father who rules the universe and every creature therein; who has a work for all to do, the object of which we shall better know by and by. Till that time comes, we will never doubt that these martyrs of religious enthusiasm suffered in a cause that was in some way acceptable to Him.

CHAPTER XIII.

THE Wasatch range, bounding Salt Lake Valley on the east, recently traversed, contains the first discovered silver-mines of Utah. But the Oquirrh or Western range, likewise running north and south on the opposite side of the basin, is now competing with it in rich production.

The description already given of Little Cottonwood applies in many respects to the cañons of the Western mountains. The scenery is alike grand and impressive, and the mining-camps embrace the same peculiarities of a distinct civilization or barbarism, according as the reader's option may define such a condition of society.

The "Salt Lake, Sevier Valley and Pioche Railroad" is another illustration of the enterprises already undertaken and rapidly progressing in Utah. This work is intended to open some of the most important silver, coal, and iron mining, as well as the rich agricultural districts in the western and southern parts of the Territory, of which I shall say more in a subsequent chapter. Like the Utah " Northern," " Central," and " Southern," this road will not only be a good investment for its stockholders, but will eventually contribute largely to the profit of the great trunk lines of the " Union " and " Central " Pacific.

The whole distance from Salt Lake City to the point of its completion will be three hundred and thirty-six miles, and its cost is estimated at less than six millions of dollars. It is neither an exclusively Mormon nor a Gentile undertaking. Its chief projector is H. S. Jacobs, Esq., who, though a Gentile, has long resided in Salt Lake City. He and his eastern associates are working harmoniously with the Saints for the development of the country, irrespective of religious prejudices. What wonderful peacemakers and civilizers are railroads! How they give the lie to that party clamor which, in the name of philanthropy, would destroy the prosperity of this community!

Since I passed over the ground about to be described, twenty-two miles of this railroad have been finished and equipped. The stage-line will soon be entirely superseded.

We drove to Ophir on the stage-coach, along the line of the new railroad, leaving Salt Lake City at an early hour in the morning, passing through a well-cultivated region for a few miles, and then crossing the sage-brush desert until we reached the northern limit of the Oquirrh Mountains, where the Great Salt Lake washes their base. A road has been cut around the cliff at this point with much ingenuity.

We were now in another valley—the Tooele—bounded still by another range, the Ophir, on the west, and on the north by the lake, along the borders of which our road now lay. A fresh northerly breeze had ruffled its surface, the rollers were combing and dashing their spray upon the beach; the salty breath of the wind was on our faces, and altogether, with the sandy plain at our feet and the northern view bounded by the horizon of the waters, the illusion was so complete that it was difficult to believe that we were not upon the shores of the ocean.

Rocky Point is a favorite place of summer resort for the citizens of the metropolis, and there is, to all appearance, a well-kept hotel and good bathing accommodation at this place. A steamer of 300 tons, originally intended for business now taken away by the railroad, makes occasional excursion trips.

Some weeks previously I embraced the opportunity of the Fourth-of-July holiday to take a cruise. Unfortunately it was not very extended, as we lost our rudder soon after starting, and so, having described a great many small circles, were obliged to return without seeing much variety. The lake extends nearly one hundred miles from north to south, with an average of forty miles from east to west. It is so intensely salt that nothing excepting a sort of small winged shrimp can live in it.

For bathing it is perfectly safe. One cannot drown in it. The water is so dense that I have tried in vain to reach the bottom, where the depth was only two fathoms. On coming out, the body is so completely encrusted with salt that the sensation is like that which may be supposed to be produced from rolling in nettles. Fresh-water ablution after a bath is a necessity.

Nearly half-way across the valley, at a distance of ten miles from either range, the Oquirrh and the Ophir, is the city of Tooele. It is literally an oasis in the desert. From far away it seems like a little green patch of grass. As we approach it its proportions are enlarged, and when we enter it we find a miniature Salt Lake City, like it in its wide streets, with streams of water, and houses and gardens on each side, and, like all the Mormon cities, exceedingly quiet and neat.

While we were changing horses I strayed into the grounds of a house near by. The proprietor was an Englishman, the lady—she might have been one by herself, or one of many—was a rosy-cheeked English-woman. They gave me some fine peaches and plums, and as they were sociably inclined, they gave me also some of their religious " experience." They were fully impressed with the divine character of what they termed their " blessed religion," and, like all other Mormons, they had the most implicit faith in Brigham Young.

A few miles beyond, we came to the small town of Stockton, which derives its subsistence from smelting the ore brought to it from the mines. After experiencing a tremendous thunder-storm of a grandness we could not but admire, although by it we were soaked with rain and pelted with hail and almost blinded by lightning, we were right glad to dry our clothes at the fire of the hotel-kitchen, and to abandon our temperance principles at the bar.

It was late when we entered the narrow Ophir Cañon, and wound up its steep and tortuous ascent, with perpendicular precipices of two thousand feet on either side. We were not sorry to reach a wooden shanty, which in reality was all it pretended to be with its French sign, in this wilderness, "Café et Hotel Restaurant," kept by Monsieur Simon. He, with Madame Simon and the little belle-sœur Elise, were fresh from Paris, and were trying to keep up Parisian style in the mountains of Utah, menu, white apron, white cap and all, not forgetting what can never be had out of France, excepting at the hands of a Frenchman, a good cup of coffee.

On the following day, crossing over to Dry Cañon with a guide, I ascended the mountains and travelled diligently from daylight till dark like a chamois, over the ledges and steeps, admiring the wonderfully grand scenery, and looking into the various mines.

Some of them are the Tiger, the Silver Chief, the Zella, the Lion, Defiance, Sunny Side, Miner's Delight, Hidden Treasure, Poor Man's Friend, Utah Queen. But the most productive and most celebrated are the Mono and Chicago.

One of the most promising of the new investments is the " Kelley Consolidated Mining and Smelting Company." This mine, with a well-defined vein of six feet, has a shaft and three tunnels already in operation, and the smelting furnaces are about commencing work. It is principally owned and managed by Col. Kelley, a New York gentleman of much practical experience, who is fairly counting on splendid results.

This mine was discovered several years ago by a poor German named Hirsch. He worked away at it, starving himself to employ necessary assistance, and then selling his ore to develop still further with the proceeds. At last he sold his property to Col. Kelley for a very high price, which would enable him to live in luxury for all his remaining days.

But now he insists that the little hut, half stone, half log, in which he has lived the life of a hermit for so many winters and summers, shall remain his property, for he cannot live anywhere else! Here then he will remain, prospecting for another mine. He has mining upon the brain. He can think or talk of nothing else. Mines are the idols to which he is joined, and he prefers to be let alone.

Coming out of Ophir Cañon and pursuing the same route by which we had entered through Tooele Valley as far as the lake, we rounded the mountain point and kept along the eastern base of the Oquirrh range until we came to the opening of Bingham Cañon.

This is a comparatively new mining district, bidding fair to rival any of the others in production of large quantities of ore. The quality is generally not so rich as in the Cottonwood district, but this is compensated for by its abundance. The average assay may be calculated at forty per cent. lead and forty ounces of silver to the ton. It is generally considered that this percentage of lead pays all expenses of whatever kind in mining, freight, and smelting ; and thus that all the silver extracted is clear profit.

The " Last Chance " is one of the most productive mines, paying an annual dividend of twenty per cent.

on $250,000, the sum for which it was sold ; and the "Crœsus" and "Jerry" in the same neighborhood are likely soon to rival it.

The village of Bingham, five miles within the cañon, is remarkable for nothing especially different from other mining camps already described, excepting that murders are rather more common.   A few days before our arrival there was a lively family difficulty, in which a father and his three sons were killed.   Their relations contemplate shooting the murderer when they catch him, and as in that case the murderer's friends will "go for" them, and as that "going for" will be avenged, there is likely to be a diminution of the population of the camp.

Bingham is a healthy locality as to climate, but there are other influences which make life quite as insecure as where yellow fever and cholera prevail. Whiskey kills a great many people, not accounted for, in the little cemetery, as murdered.   The number of headstones telling of violent death by the pistol and knife is quite appalling.   "The burying-ground is getting to be a little respectable now.   There's two fellers in there," said my informant, "who died a nat'ral death—all the rest of 'em would have been alive now if they'd kept clear of whiskey and lived peaceable."

The scenery of this cañon is very picturesque,

although it can scarcely compare with that of the valleys of the opposite range. The railroad being graded from Bingham Cañon to Sandy has now been completed and is in running order. It is on the narrow-gauge or three-feet pattern, like the Utah Northern. Its heaviest grade where it mounts the cañon is 230 feet to the mile. Had it been desirable, the distance from Bingham to Salt Lake City might have been materially shortened ; but it was for the advantage of the mining interest to have it intersect the Utah Southern at a point twelve miles south of the city : thus the mining and smelting works are brought into close relations. Its entire length is eighteen miles, and, as most of the track is on a level plain, the cost of the work is small. Especially is it so, in comparison with the large business reasonably anticipated. The company was organized under the laws of Utah in the autumn of 1872 ; the road was commenced in the spring of 1873, and opened for business on the 1st of December last. Its present equipment consists of two locomotives and ninety-two cars. The whole cost of the road and rolling-stock is not far from $400,000.

For the three winter months $21,000 have been the gross receipts, and of course a large and increasing business is anticipated in the summer season.

Bingham Cañon has this advantage over Little Cot

tonwood the region of the Emma and other valuable mines on the Wasatch range, that the operation of the mines is not impeded by snow.

The entrance of the cañon is twenty-five miles from Salt Lake City. Distances are so deceptive in this rarefied atmosphere, that on emerging at the plain it seemed that only a few miles were before us until we should reach the beautiful city so clearly distinguished nestling under the Wasatch Mountains.

Surrounded as every dwelling is by garden-trees, the appearance was rather that of a forest dotted here and there with white houses. Certainly Salt Lake City from any point is beautiful, and it never looked more lovely than as we approached it on this bright September afternoon.

I have often wondered why a more euphonious name was not selected by its founder. He has called the river running through the plains the Jordan, and has rechristened many other localities from the Bible. Why did he not call the capital of his Zion the New Jerusalem? He might well have named the Utah fresh-water lake, from which the Jordan takes its rise the Sea of Galilee, and the Great Salt Lake into which it flows the Dead Sea; for the geographical similarity is exact. Perhaps, if it is not too late, he may take the hint even from an unbelieving Gentile.

CHAPTER XIV.

The Mormon Religion—History of Joseph Smith.—The Book of Mormon.—Mormon Migrations.—Brigham Young.—His Enterprises and his Character.

THE religion of the " Latter-Day Saints " may be defined as a compound of Judaism and Christianity, with additions and subtractions. It is an attempt to roll the world back to the days of that barbarism styled " primitive simplicity," and to work up civilization from the Mosaic basis with the help of the Gospel of Christ, arrogating for the new church another monopoly of the Divine protection.

Since the Christian era many false prophets have appeared upon the stage, Mahomet the most successful of them all. In these last days Joseph Smith has endeavored to emulate him, and, like him, has started his new religion with dreams, adopting, moreover, one of the practical doctrines of Mahometanism.

The history of the first Mormon Apostle was developed in fanaticism, and culminated in imposture. In 1820, Smith, then a boy of fifteen years of age, became the subject of a religious revival, was half-crazed with solicitude for his salvation, and in one of his seasons of insane excitement actually supposed himself the recipient of angelic visits.

He was doubtless sincere for a time, but afterwards concluded to make the reputation of a prophet that he had gained, available for business purposes. In 1823 this precocious youth had another vision, in which he was directed to proceed to the top of a hill in Ontario County, New York, where he would find buried a box of golden plates, with a new revelation engraved upon them. He went as divinely directed, found the plates, and was about to remove them, when the angel appeared and told him to leave them there for four years, and then to come and take them.

Joseph says that he waited patiently until the "set time" came round, working on a farm and getting married to his first wife. When this set time had come he went to the hill again, and the angel was kind enough to dig up the plates and to place them in his hands.

These golden slabs were inscribed with unknown characters, but, with the assistance of the angel and a confederate, Joseph translated them into the English of the time of King James, in which language, by-the-by, all Mormon revelations have been and are still given.

I asked a Mormon gentleman, who should be a

man of intelligence, for he is a librarian in Salt
Lake City, how it happened that the angel's English
was so antique? "Of course," he replied, "it was
natural that it should be so. That is the kind of language in which God revealed himself to his ancient
people!" I remember once hearing a good scriptural New England lady trying to prove her favorite
doctrines of original sin and total depravity from St.
Paul's assertion that "by one man's disobedience
many were made sinners;" and when I ventured to
suggest that "made" did not mean created, referring
to the original for evidence, she cut me short by ex-
claiming, "I don't want to hear anything about your
Hebrew or Greek; the good old English Bible is good
enough for me!"

Joe Smith was well aware of the reverence attached
to such phrases as "Verily, verily," and "Behold,
it came to pass." The translation of these supposed
plates is "The Book of Mormon." It purports to be
chiefly a history of the lost tribes of Israel, who are
found to have drifted over to America when separated
from the tribes of Judah, and it is, besides, an expo-
sition of the new doctrine of the church.

There are two theories accounting for this production. One is, that it was a religious novel written
for his own amusement by a retired clergyman named
Solomon Spalding, of which Smith the prophet be-

came feloniously possessed ; and the other is, that Smith, whose mind was stored with Scripture phrases, being still under the delusion that he was divinely inspired, actually wrote and dictated the book in a condition of clairvoyant insanity.

Without any pretence of clairvoyance or of spiritual communication, Mr. Dickens has declared that every word put in the mouths of his characters was mysteriously but distinctly heard by him.   In such a case of clairvoyant manifestation as this, Smith may have really found the plates as he professed he did, which is not impossible, similar ancient and undeciphered tablets having been more recently discovered in the mounds of Ohio.   Although it is very nearly certain that Spalding was the author of the book, yet, in the absence of positive proof, Joe Smith is entitled to the benefit of this construction.

At any rate, Smith maintained his assertion that he had received the plates from the angel till the day of his death, and imagined himself to be a prophet and a martyr.   But his revelations received from time to time suited his own convenience most wonderfully.

Polygamy was not an original doctrine of Mormonism, but was revealed to Smith to meet some difficulties of a social character with which he found himself embarrassed.

The " Church of the Latter-Day Saints " was organized in Fayette, Seneca County, New York, April 6, 1830, and consisted of six members, who laid their hands upon each other and gave themselves the gift of the Holy Ghost. A new revelation commanded the church soon afterwards to remove to Kirtland, Ohio. Thence they were ordered to Missouri, where Jackson County was designated as the promised land. Here they suffered all manner of persecutions, and were finally driven out.

They took refuge in Illinois, where they founded the city of Nauvoo. They had scarcely finished their magnificent temple there, when, after repeated troubles with their neighbors, in which, as in Missouri, they were undeniably in the right, they were finally expelled, the prophet and his brother being killed by the mob. He foretold his own death, and whatever may have been the inconsistencies of his life, he met his end heroically, and died in the full conviction of his divine mission. This was in 1844.

Brigham Young became his successor, and, in obedience to the order of the murdered prophet, led the Mormon hosts, when driven from Nauvoo, to the far West, advancing step by step till they reached Council Bluffs on the Missouri River, and thence making their great exodus to Salt Lake Valley, where, as has been stated, they finally arrived on the 24th of July, 1847.

Joseph Smith was a half-crazed boy Methodist when he imagined himself to be divinely inspired. Brigham Young was in the prime of manhood when at the age of thirty-two he determined to enlist under the banner of the prophet. He was a sharp, clear-headed Yankee. He originally " went in for a good thing," and he has proved himself a man of most consummate tact and business ability, fertile in conception, ready in expedients, and successful in carrying out almost every enterprise he has undertaken.

Joseph Smith was regarded by his followers as a prophet of the Lord, pure and simple, and, in the earlier part of his career, a dispenser of heavenly mysteries alone. Brigham Young, who is wise as a serpent if not quite as harmless as a dove, has their confidence not only in everything pertaining to heaven above, but on the earth beneath.

He is a priest and king, bishop and farmer, minister and manufacturer—theoretical in religion and practical in all the affairs of life. When he has a revelation of a new doctrine, the people believe it. When he counsels a new mode of irrigation, they dig the ditch. When he preaches morality, they practise it, and when he wants woollen-mills and railroads, they build them.

It is true they complain of the burden of tithes, but they pay or apostatize. Almost all the apostacy can be traced to this source, and it is wonderful that

there is no more, and that despite this great incen-
tive to rebel against his authority, this authority is so
little questioned by nine-tenths of the population of
Utah.

There is about him a certain magnetism of person
and character which commands respect and love from
all classes of his people, notwithstanding his occasional coarseness and vulgarity.   He is a man of very
limited education, deficient in grammatical speech and
orthography, but of the most varied information on
all subjects of practical importance.   He is a close
and successful student of human nature, and does not
neglect books.

In his choice and excellent library I saw many vol-
umes of history and political economy, of English
classics, and works of the best American writers ; but I
looked in vain for Hebrew and Greek literature, to
which, although it is pretended that he sometimes
"speaks in unknown tongues," he has not directed his
attention.

He would fain have isolated Utah from the rest of
the world, but when he found that to be impossible,
he manfully accepted the situation, and made the
world pay him for its intrusion.   "Let the Gentiles
work the mines," he tells his people, "they are uncertain investments ; but we will build railroads to carry
coal, lumber, and food to them, and to transport their

ore, and we will raise wheat to feed them. This is certain profit."

He has established a co-operative system of trade unequalled in skilful working and beneficial results. The headquarters of the "Zion's Co-operative Mercantile Institution," with its great sign, "Holiness to the Lord," is in Salt Lake City, and its branches shoot out into every settlement of the Territory. By prudent and honest management it is made not only to afford articles of every description more cheaply to the people at large than they can be purchased elsewhere, but to pay an annual dividend to the stockholders of fifteen to twenty per cent. It is no monopoly, for single shares are distributed generally. He superintends it himself, as he likewise looks after the banking interests of the church.

While his promise to the faithful of blessings in the other world are of an extraordinary and doubtful character, he is evidently instructing them how they can make this world turn to their advantage. On one Sunday he may tell them how they can get a greater "exaltation" in heaven, but on ten Sundays he will tell them how to irrigate and drain land, harvest crops, build fences, set out trees, beautify their grounds, raise cattle, saw lumber, and manufacture cloth; and this is the character of the sermons most frequently preached by the clergy.

I am, perhaps, wrong in using this word. The Mormons have no clergy, as distinct from the people. The highest apostle among them, like St. Paul, works at his trade. It would be a novelty to see a Catholic or an Anglican bishop hoeing his corn or driving his ox-team; but this is not unusual for the Mormon bishops, and Brigham Young has set them the example.

I have intimated a doubt of his sincerity in first joining the church, for I think he should have been too shrewd a man to believe in the miracles or divine mission of Joe Smith; but however that may be, I am half inclined to think that he has convinced himself that he is inspired. He may have vivid dreams, which he honestly supposes to be revelations. It must be admitted, however, that these revelations are, like those of Smith, very convenient and well adapted to the policy of the occasion.

In Utah he is generally called a good man. Elsewhere he is almost invariably called bad. In reviewing his history we cannot touch upon his motives. These are known only to God and to himself, but he must be judged by his acts and their consequences. These are both bad and good. He has retaliated upon his enemies by treating them harshly and perhaps with cruelty, but the provocation should be taken into account. On the other hand, he has done much good for his own people. He has been accused of instigating, if not of absolutely perpetrating, brutal murders in years past; but there is no warrant for believing this, while it is undoubtedly true that he would not allow the interests of the church to suffer by bringing the offenders to justice.

Is he an out-and-out hypocrite? By no means. Is he always sincere? Facts are rather adverse to this supposition. Is he a great man? Yes, he is; and history will one day record that among all impostors or leaders of new sects, Brigham Young has been one of the most successful, if not in pointing out the true road to heaven, at least in heading a new civilization, which, with all its errors in practice—and they will soon disappear—has drawn together tens of thousands of people and made them happier and more prosperous on this earth than they ever were before.

CHAPTER XV.

OF the Mormon sect it may be truly said, as of every other Christian organization, and of Christianity itself, that "the blood of the Martyrs is the seed of the Church." If Mormonism had been left to itself, it would have died like thousands of other wild extravagances that have cropped out in the ages, expiring from want of the air stirred up by the fan of persecution.

It was a harmless little beast in its infancy, but its enemies evoked the spirit of the devil wherewith to defend itself.

What could be more simple and inoffensive than the creed promulgated by Joe Smith in 1842 ?

1. We believe in God, the eternal Father, and in His Son, Jesus Christ, and in the Holy Ghost.
2. We believe that men will be punished for their own sins, and not for Adam's transgression.
3. We believe that through the atonement of Christ

all mankind may be saved by obedience to the laws and ordinances of the Gospel.

4. We believe that these ordinances are : first, Faith in the Lord Jesus Christ ; second, Repentance ; third, Baptism by immersion for the remission of sins ; fourth, Laying on of hands for the gift of the Holy Ghost.

5. We believe that a man must be called of God by " prophecy and by laying on of hands " by those who are in authority to preach the Gospel, and administer in the ordinances thereof.

6. We believe in the same organization that existed in the primitive church, viz.: apostles, prophets, pastors, teachers, evangelists, etc., etc.

7. We believe in the gift of tongues, prophecy, revelation, visions, healing, interpretations of tongues, etc.

8. We believe the Bible to be the word of God, as far as it is translated correctly. We also believe the Book of Mormon to be the word of God.

9. We believe all that God has revealed, and that He does now reveal, and we believe that He will yet reveal many great and important things pertaining to the Kingdom of God.

10. We believe in the literal gathering of Israel and of the restoration of the Ten Tribes ; that Zion will be built upon this continent ; that Christ will reign personally upon the earth, and that the earth will be renewed and receive its Paradisiac glory.

11. We claim the privilege of worshipping Almighty God according to the dictates of our conscience, and allow all men the same privilege, let them worship how, where, or what they may.

12. We believe in being subject to kings, presidents, rulers, and magistrates, in obeying, honoring, and sustaining the law.

13. We believe in being honest, true, chaste, benev-

olent, virtuous, and in doing good to all men ; indeed we may say that we follow the admonition of Paul, "We believe all things, hope all things." We have endured many things, and hope to be able to endure all things. If there is anything virtuous, lovely, or of good report or praiseworthy, we seek after these things.   JOSEPH SMITH.

Why, even the Evangelical Alliance, that refused to spread its holy skirts over Roman Catholics, because they believe too much, and over Unitarians because they believe too little, could scarcely have objected to receive the Mormons into their fold !

The ninth article is the only one which really means mischief to society. This has opened the door to innovations which have pushed Mormonism into such a remote corner of Christ's vineyard that it is unknown as still a part of it to those who walk in its beaten paths.

In accordance with the faith expressed in Article 9, " Many great and important things pertaining to the kingdom of God " have been since revealed, and there is still room for more revelations.

Some of the new doctrines are harmless enough, and the only ones which really clash with outside civilization, and come in contact with the laws of the land, are those of " blood-atonement " and polygamy.

One of the most absurd—on which I heard a most

elaborate sermon preached—is that of "baptism for the dead." The text was 1st Corinthians, xv. 29 : " Else what shall they do, which are baptized for the dead, if the dead rise not at all ? Why, are they then baptized for the dead ?"

As this text has always been a puzzle for theologians of every stripe, it was for the Mormons to have a " revelation " which should unravel it. So it was revealed that all baptisms since the time of the apostles until the advent of Joe Smith being null and void, the only way in which the intervening genera- tions could inherit salvation is by the proxy baptism of their descendants.

Devout Mormons accordingly are critical students of genealogy, hunting up their ancestors as far back as possible, and getting repeatedly immersed to· save their souls.

Alas, how few can trace beyond their grandparents ! Many cannot go into antiquity beyond their fathers, and there are unfortunate people who cannot look backwards even so far as that. At best, some proud Briton is able to prove that his progenitors " came over with William the Conqueror."

In such a family an extraordinary number of souls may be rescued from purgatory by the repeated im- mersions of their descendants. But even in these cases the intervening generations for many hundred

years must perish.   How much more sad is the fate
of the great average of Mormon ancestry !

The next doctrine in the order of absurdity, and
one closely allied to the foregoing, is that of proxy-
marriage for the dead.   The marriage ceremony,
since the days of the apostles, having been performed
by priests who had not received the proper " laying-
on of hands," is considered invalid, and consequently
all the progeny of the people so united is illegitimate
in the eye of Heaven.

But this reproach is to be taken away by a process
somewhat similar to the baptism for the dead.   The
Mormon of the present is to stand up and be married
for his ancestors, and thus.make their marriages legal.
The confused condition of society which has heretofore existed in the spirit-world will be brought into
order.   Husbands and wives who have been separated for fifteen or sixteen centuries will be reunited,
and will again beget children in heaven ; for it is a
Mormon tenet that marriages contracted by Latter-
Day Saints on earth, or those thus legalized above,
are eternally continuous—that men and women there
have the same flesh and blood of which they are here
made, and are possessed of the same animal natures.

Consequently the propagation of the human race
will be continued, and as myriads of new beings are
thus called into existence, new worlds upon worlds

will be created for their occupation, and this reproduction of men and worlds will continue throughout
eternity.

There are innumerable vagaries besides these into
which run the crazy imaginations of the prophets, induced by dreams, begotten perhaps by indigestion,
but which they call visions or revelations.

Many of their doctrines are so materialistic that
they seem blasphemous to us.   Founding their belief
on the declaration of the Almighty that He would
make men " after His own image," they say that
the great First Cause is Himself a being of flesh and
blood ; so is Christ, and so is the Holy Ghost ; so are
all the Angels, and so are all the redeemed among
men.

" God," they say, was literally " the father of our
Lord Jesus Christ."   Christ himself was, although a
divine being, a married man—and Martha and Mary
were His wives because " He loved them "—and He
must have had children ; " for who shall declare His
generation ? "

These and other wild extravagances are the results
of that pernicious article ninth of Joe Smith's creed,
which allows future revelations to instil new doctrines.
The Book of Mormon, chiefly purporting to be a
history, does not authorize them.   They are all
modern improvements.

Now, I do not suppose that it is of the least possible consequence to other people whether the Mormons continue to believe or renounce them. It is no man's business what another man believes, so long as that belief is not practically injurious to society. The only thing which concerns us is that the life and property of every man, woman, and child, so far as the laws of the United States can control them, shall be as secure in Utah as in any other State or Territory of the Union,—and they are.

The "blood-atonement" is no more advocated as it once was in the Mormon pulpit. When it was preached and practised to such a fearful extent as formerly, it was a barbarism worse than slavery or polygamy. No man's life was safe under its rule. It was held justifiable to slay an apostate—not, remember, from revenge, but for the good of his own soul! Nay, more, apostates who desired to return to the church, and others who had committed deadly offences, often had upon their consciences such weights of unforgiven sin, that despairing of heaven without the "remission by the shedding of blood," they have surrendered themselves to be sacrificed by their friends; and these wretched fanatics have murdered their brothers to save their souls!

A most horrible, and I fear too true a story, is told of a refined and beautiful woman in Salt Lake City who had been unfaithful to her husband, and who came to him confessing her sin, obtained his forgiveness, gave and received a farewell kiss, and then he coolly cut her throat in order that the blood-atonement might procure for her " an exaltation," and that they might be again united in heaven !

Fortunately, this horrible doctrine, having escaped the notice of politicians and newspapers in their attention to polygamy, is dying a natural death. In years gone by it has been the instigator of great wrong and suffering.

CHAPTER XVI.

The Mountain Meadows Massacre.—The Battle with the Morrisites.—
" Let us have peace."

THE Mormon nature, like that of a hound which has once tasted blood, has been on occasions ferocious. The " Mountain Meadows Massacre " of 1857 is one of the saddest recorded instances of barbarous fanaticism.

A company of emigrants of one hundred and twenty men, women, and children, on their way to California, were passing through Utah. Heretofore, and generally afterwards, the emigrants were kindly treated by the Mormons, whose interest it was to exchange with them provisions for money and articles of trade. But in this case, merely because it was conjectured that among their number there were two or three individuals who had persecuted the Saints while they were settled in Missouri, vengeance was taken on the whole company.

Brigham Young then held the commission of Governor from the President of the United States.

It is said, and I do not know that it has been denied by him, that he sent orders to all the settlements to withhold supplies from this company, and to have no intercourse with them whatever. If this be true, it should have been the cause of his instant removal from office; for it was equivalent to an attempt to starve them, and was in any point of view a criminal offence in an officer of the government.

After unsuccessful attempts to procure provisions, the company moved on to the West; but before they had got beyond the confines of Utah, they were attacked by a large force of Indians and Mormons disguised as Indians, and every individual, with the exception of seventeen little children, was murdered in cold blood!

It is scarcely pretended that Brigham Young gave the order for this massacre, but it is a fact that he took no steps to bring the perpetrators to punishment. The band of murderers was undoubtedly made up of savages, thieves, and zealots, and the crime may be imputed to them all. But no one can deny that Mormonism is entitled to its share. This is the most horrid story in all the annals of Utah.

Next in order is the butchery of the Morrisites in 1862. Morris was a fanatic who had the audacity to have revelations at variance with those given by the Lord to Brigham Young. He was instructed by the

Lord to warn Brigham himself that he was going to too great an excess in matrimony.

The prophet, of course, did not credit the divine mission of Morris, nor did he like to be instructed by him ; but he treated him with sublime indifference. At last Morris, growing bold, rendered himself amenable to the civil law, and, after many disputes, he and his followers took up arms and entrenched themselves in their fortified settlement.

Here they were attacked by the Mormon forces, and their surrender demanded. Retiring into their " bowery," the summer meeting-house in general use, they commenced praying to the Lord for counsel. Then the Mormons fired on them, killing several persons and severely wounding others. Among them was a little girl whom I afterwards met at Soda Springs. She is now a married woman, and her scarred face is a memorial of that day. From herself and her husband, who was also present, I received this account.

The men rushed to their arms, and defended themselves, their families, and their property for three days, when their ammunition was exhausted. Then, under the protection of a white flag, they surrendered and Burton, the leader of the attacking party, riding up to Morris, shot him dead, and when two women thereupon called him a bloodthirsty wretch, this modern Claverhouse shot them dead likewise ! Thus

did he make a "blood-atonement" for the wretched
Morrisites and saved their souls!

Happily, these atrocities are things of the past.
They proceeded from a curious mixture of human
passion and religious fanaticism, superinduced by remembrance of the persecutions which they themselves had suffered. "Vengeance is mine, saith the
Lord," but the Mormons, supposing that they, like
the Israelites, were his peculiar people, considered
themselves deputed by him to carry out his behests.
In their view, all who interfered with them were
Canaanites, Jebusites, Hittites, and Amalekites, and
if Joshua and the armies of Israel smote these troublesome neighbors by tens of thousands at a time, they
really did not think they had done anything wrong in
killing a few Gentiles and heretics, especially when—
what never entered into Joshua's plans—their souls
were to be saved by "the shedding of blood!"

I do not remember the name of the Federal officer
to whom some deputation recently came with a long
string of grievances and an enumeration of outrages
committed by the Mormons. "Have any of these
things been done within a year?" he asked. "No."
"Within two, three, four, or five years?" "No."
"Well," he replied, "if they have kept the peace so
long, we can trust them now without looking into the
past."

CHAPTER XVII.

Polygamy.—Orson Pratt's Discourse on Marriage.—Mormon Arguments in favor of Polygamy.

THE *bête noire* now agitating the public mind is polygamy, which is still prevalent in Utah, although it does not exist to the extent generally supposed. Probably through the territory one man out of five or six may have more than one wife. In some settlements a polygamic family cannot be found at all.

When, as is seen by the last census, there are more males than females in the Territory, it must be admitted that the natural tendencies are against it.

It is well enough to make a distinction, which is not always allowed, between sin and crime. If I remember aright my old Assembly's Catechism, " Sin is any want of conformity to, or transgression of, the Law of God." Now the Law of God is imprinted differently on different consciences ; whereas crime, which is an offence against the law of the land, is printed clearly and distinctly, so that the characters are legible to all alike. Polygamy to those of us who pin our faith on the New Testament is a sin ; to the Latter-Day Saints, who

imagine their church a reproduction of Judaism to a
great extent, and who consequently rely quite as
much on the Old Testament as on the New, it may be
no sin, but for them as well as for us it is a crime,
because bigamy is an offence against the common
law.

"Sin," says Shenstone, "does not consist in any
deviation from received opinion ; it does not depend
upon the understanding, but the will.   Now, if it appear that a man's opinion has happened to misplace
his duty, and this opinion has not been owing to any
vicious desire of indulging his appetites—in short, if
his own reason, liable to err, has biased his will, rather
than his will contributed to bias and deprave his
reason, he will perhaps appear guilty before none beside an earthly tribunal."   I commend the casuistry
of this old essayist to the candid consideration of my
Mormon friends.   If any one of them can truly say
that he is a polygamist not " owing to any vicious
desire of indulging his appetites," then he is merely
a criminal, not a sinner.

Orson Pratt preached a discourse on marriage while
I was at Salt Lake, and fortunately on that day I
happened to be present at the Tabernacle.   This
apostle is the most eloquent of all the brotherhood.
He is a man of fine appearance and of such a logical
turn of mind that he was selected to enter the lists

against the Rev. Dr. Newman when he came to Salt Lake for the purpose of showing the Mormons the error of their ways.

In this sermon he laid down these propositions: "Baptism is a religious sacrament; marriage is a religious sacrament. Congress will not pretend to legislate for baptism. It will not ordain how a man shall be baptized, whether he shall be sprinkled or immersed, or how much he shall be sprinkled or immersed. What right, then, has Congress to legislate about marriage? What right has it to say how we shall be married, or how much we shall be married?"

He then went on to the threadbare argument of patriarchal polygamy, showing how it was practised by those holy men who are supposed to have been especial favorites with the Almighty.

"Now," said he, "I will suppose myself to be a Gentile, and at my death in some way I have attained heaven—the heaven all Christians desire when they talk of 'sitting down with Abraham and Isaac and Jacob in the Kingdom of God.' Well, the angel opens for me one of the pearly gates of Paradise, and I am about to walk in and take my place, when my eye rests upon Jacob sitting there with his four wives, Leah, Rachel, Bilhah, and Zilpah, with all their children. I draw back in disgust, and tell the angel that I cannot sit down near that old polygamist!

"Well, the angel kindly shows me in at another gate. But there I see David, 'the man after God's own heart,' and Solomon, the man whom He endowed with celestial wisdom; I see them with crowds of wives and hundreds of children. 'Worse and worse,' I tell the angel; 'I won't go in there. Is there no other place for me?'

"'Oh yes,' replies my divine conductor, 'there is plenty of room for you outside, "for without are dogs, and sorcerers, and whoremongers, and murderers, and idolaters, and whosoever loveth and maketh a lie." I think that is the place that will just suit such particular people as you!' And so I am obliged to put up with the society of God's favorites, or with that of the devil's imps!"

"What do you think of the sermon?" asked a Mormon gentleman, as we walked home from the Tabernacle. "Wasn't it all scriptural?"

"Yes," I replied, "it was; and so if Mr. Pratt had told you to sacrifice your son, as Abraham proposed to do, or to immolate your daughter, as Jephtha actually did, would you feel justified in obeying?" "Yes, I suppose so," he replied, after a little hesitation, "if it's Scripture." "Well, it is Scripture," I answered— "Old Testament Scripture—good enough Scripture for those times, but which will not stand the test of modern civilization. If Abraham lived in these days, and sharpened his knife to slay his son, we would put him in a lunatic asylum; and as to Jephtha, we would hang him—if the jury did not disagree, or find him guilty of forgery or petit larceny. Just so with your polygamy. The law of the land is against it. Anywhere else you would be convicted of bigamy. Only here, fortunately for you, no jury would bring in such a verdict."

Rev. Dr. Newman, and all such men, make a great mistake in discussing polygamy on its religious merits, unless they are willing to throw the Old Testament overboard altogether—at least that part of it which they cannot disprove.

While advocating its abolition as soon as natural causes will bring it about, without detriment to the happiness and welfare of families, the good of society, and the peace of the country, I am forced to admit that its consequences are not altogether so horrible as they are often represented to be.

There is nothing so good that it may not be abused, neither is there anything so bad that it may not be of some use. Polygamy is surely bad enough, but the Mormons claim for it this merit: it annihilates what is called the " social evil,". by making comparatively respectable women of girls who might otherwise be prostitutes. This vice, excepting in communities largely composed of Gentiles, does not exist in Utah, and even there it is kept down by Mormon territorial and municipal law.

The women themselves are not averse to polygamy. Among the working classes in the country they say it promotes a division of labor. The Utah farmer's wives do not have the over-worked air of the women of our country districts, who are obliged singly to bear all the children and to do all the work of the family.

And yet Mrs. Stenhouse would have us understand that the doctrine is universally execrated by her sex. Doubtless there are many women who are living in its practice with continual abhorrence and disgust. But it must be remembered that Mrs. Stenhouse and her husband are apostates. Like all apostates, they are inclined to unmeritedly abuse the faith they once professed. Mr. and Mrs. Stenhouse are regarded in Salt Lake City with aversion alike by Gentiles and Mormons. By their own confession they believed in the divine revelation of Mormonism, polygamy and all, with very little scruple or hesitation, until Brigham Young gave them an order to remove to Ogden for the benefit of the church, and thus to sacrifice a lucrative business.

Then all at once their eyes became opened to the enormities of a religion they had professed and practised for so many years. They found that they could gain more money by abandoning and vilifying it than by remaining its disciples. They have proved that they were either insincere throughout all their Mormon experience, or that they are insincere now.

I was astonished to hear polygamy advocated by ladies of education and refinement, among them a school-teacher who strongly favored it, perhaps because she was no longer young. At a hotel where I was staying I met a young married lady of one of the first families of Salt Lake. Two of her intimate friends were with her. One day, when they were out of the room, she asked me, "What do you think of A——?" "She is a charming girl," I replied. "Indeed she is," exclaimed Mrs. B——. "I do wish B—— (her husband) would marry her. I should so like to have her with me all the time!"

The Mormon ladies believe that in the other world a married woman arrives at a higher sphere than an unmarried one, and that one who is willing that her husband should have another wife has a still higher place. The men share in the same belief, and think that the more wives they have the happier they will be in the future.

I know a bishop who said that he really did not want to take a second wife, and his wife did not wish him to marry again, until they both prayed often and fervently over it, and at last became convinced that their eternal welfare would be promoted by the process, and then they concluded to have another woman in the family. I noticed, however, that the conscientious bishop mitigated his reluctance by selecting a young and pretty girl for his self-sacrifice and spiritual good.

Strange as it may seem, the arrangement appears to work better when the wives are sisters. It is not uncommon for a man to marry several of them. Perhaps it is for the sake of having only one mother-in-law. Unless a visitor takes up his residence in a family for some time, he cannot be a judge of its domestic happiness or misery. Even when there is only one husband and one wife, in any community "good faces are always put on before company." Most people are sensible enough to keep their private quarrels out of sight.

A henpecked Mormon may have this advantage over a Gentile. He may escape from one wife who happens to be in a bad temper to the society of another, who, for the time being, is more amiably disposed; but on the whole, he must have a hard time, for occasionally he will be obliged to stand the extraordinary pressure of them all. As to the women who elsewhere complain of having a man about them continually to torment them, they have the satisfaction of dividing his ill-nature as well as his attentions.

I was never inquisitive when visiting Mormon families. Sometimes conversation was volunteered. A very respectable gentleman in Salt Lake City remarked: "The only difference between our people and yours, is that we marry our concubines—you don't."

One argued against Gentiles, that there were many unmarried young men in Utah and yet no houses of prostitution there, while in other communities, where the same proportion of married and unmarried men existed, all of them were infested by brothels, therefore those houses must be mainly supported by the married.

A Gentile lady asked a Mormon lady, with whom she was on intimate terms, how she could bear the knowledge that her husband was passing his time with another woman? She replied, "Certainly it is not pleasant to think of, but we have this advantage over you, we know where our husbands are—you don't!" The other might have well retorted that in such a case "ignorance is bliss!"

A gentleman catechised me in this way: "What do you think of the majority of the women in Salt Lake City—do you think they are virtuous or not, it being understood that polygamy is justifiable?"

"With that exception, I believe there is no city in the world where they are more so."

" How does it compare in this respect with New
York or Boston ? "

" Most favorably."

" What are the average wages of shop-girls in those
cities ? "

" I believe about five dollars per week."

" Doesn't it cost them about that for board and
lodging ? "

" I should suppose it might."

" Where do they get their silk dresses, then ? "

" Well, there are many of them who don't have
silk dresses ; and some of them who do have them
get them honestly.   A great many of them undoubtedly do what they ought not to do."

" Yes, and wouldn't it be better for them to be No.
2, 3, or 4 in a good family here than to earn money
in that way ? "

" That's a matter of taste for those young women
to consider.   I don't think it is polygamy that keeps
your women virtuous.   It is their simple habit of
dress ; when fashion asserts its authority in Salt Lake
and takes charge of your decks, look out for breakers
ahead ! "

I have spoken of polygamy sometimes lightly, for I
have seen it chiefly in its comical aspects.   But to
treat it seriously, let us meet the Mormon arguments
squarely.   " It has the example of the patriarchs," they

s: . We repudiate the practices of those too much
v :nerated men, and fall back on the pure precepts of
Christianity.

"It prevents the prostitution of women." Allow-
ing this argument all the force it deserves, we have
already hinted that simplicity of dress is a greater safe-
guard for virtue.

"It divides the labor of the household!" Most
women would prefer all the labor and all the husband.
If woman-nature is the same that it is elsewhere,
even the hopes of a greater "exaltation" in the
other world can hardly pay for the heart-burnings
and jealousies that, despite all denial, must infallibly
torment a family of many women and one man!

It is idle to extenuate the evils of a system that
must be condemned *in toto* as a blot upon civilization, a degradation of women, and a monstrosity too
abnormal to live.

CHAPTER XVIII.

The Future of the Mormon Religion.

POLYGAMY cannot much longer survive. There are causes at work which will bring about its speedy extinction. The Congress of the United States has firmly resolved that whatever may be the increase of the population of Utah, it shall not be admitted as a State until polygamy is abolished.

Brigham Young and all those in authority are extremely desirous, for the perpetuation of their own power, that a State government shall be established. The people are already exceedingly restive under the tithing system. The ten-per-cent. income-tax for the church is becoming yearly more difficult to collect. " Pay your tithes or you cannot inherit the kingdom," has been the refrain of many sermons that I have heard.

Once a State, Utah will be more free of Federal control than it now is as a Territory, and then taxes, nominally for the State, but in some way made advantageous for the church, can be collected by law, and these not only from apostate Mormons but from

Gentiles as well. Every State, county, municipal, and town officer will be a Mormon. The judiciary will be Mormon. The public schools will be, if possible, more under Mormon influence than they now are, and the Book of Mormon will be their text-book. There is nothing in the Constitution of the United States to prevent such an exercise of State rights.

Congress having refused to admit Utah as a State to the Union until polygamy is discontinued, has virtually declared that with its abolition no objection to her admission will be offered. Naturally, the Gentile part of the population do not desire it, for they know that they will have no power or voice in the management of State affairs. The Mormons pray for it continually, and their prayers will soon be heard, for Brigham Young will ere long have another revelation. Some angel is probably already on the way to him with a new "Thus saith the Lord." In short, although he would dislike extremely to yield up a favorite doctrine, the preservation of his power and the collection of tithes are of more importance to him than the continuance of one practice alone standing in the way, and which has not the attractions for him that it once had.

Moreover, he is aware that there are other influences aiding to accomplish its overthrow. A few small sects of the Mormons in Utah are opposed to it, and

on the banks of the Missouri the church of the Latter-
Day Saints is being revived in its original purity by
the son of its founder. This society is sending its
missionaries into the country, and their influence is
widely felt.

There are Gentile missionaries, too, earnestly at
work, not of the "American Board," or of the
proselyting sect of the Rev. Dr. Newman, but more
mighty than these, the priestesses of fashion—milli-
ners and dressmakers.

These come to Salt Lake City, and display their
gospels in the shop windows, and conversions are
miraculous. Despite all the anathemas of Brigham
Young, the Mormon women are becoming fond of
jaunty hats, ribbons, and expensive silks. His own
wives and daughters indulge in those worldly vanities
to an alarming extent. Powerful as he is in council
and in all else, he cannot control a woman's love of
finery and extravagance.

So far as he is concerned it does not matter. He is
rich and can afford it. But alas for the man of moderate means! When woman ceases to be a help-meet
for him, and becomes only an expensive toy to be kept
in ornamental repair, how shall he support more than
one wife? I say it seriously, this solves the question
of polygamy.

But what of Mormonism when this stain upon it is

erased? It will be stronger than ever.   No other sects of Christians can populate this territory in the same ratio.   The miners and traders, who come here with little enthusiasm for religion of any kind, are comparatively few in number, are without families, and seldom remain permanently.

Nearly one hundred and fifty thousand Mormons are already in Utah and the adjoining territories. Missionaries are spreading their faith in all directions, and a union will probably soon be formed with the followers of the younger Smith.   The immigration from the Eastern continent, now coming in by thousands, will be increased immeasurably.

When I remember what I have seen in the North of Europe, among the Scandinavian nations from whom the Saints are so largely recruited, how wretchedly ignorant, enslaved, and brutalized they are in their old homes; and compare this with what I have witnessed of the intelligent freedom, industry, sobriety and happiness of those who have emigrated to Utah; when I see how, notwithstanding all its defects and even barbarisms, the Mormon faith, where it has supreme control, has utterly abolished intemperance, gambling, licentiousness, and general immorality, I cannot regret the existence of a religion that has conferred such benefits upon humanity.

In due time, if their growth is not encouraged by

the stimulus of persecution and political agitation, all the excrescences of Mormonism will be lopped off, the poisonous vines that still cling to it will die a natural death, and the tree itself will live with others " to bear the peaceable fruits of righteousness" in the garden of God.

CHAPTER XIX.

A T present a great deal of the ore as it comes roughly from the silver mines is shipped over the Utah Central and Union Pacific Roads, to the East, and some of it finds its way to New York, where it is refined, or whence it is shipped to England. Much of the coarser kind is shipped by the Central Pacific to San Francisco, and thence by sailing-vessels to Europe, the shorter distance by rail making a lesser freight counterbalance the loss of time. A very large portion of the ore, however, goes East, and is delivered at Pittsburgh, where the cheapness of coal and coke converts it into bullion on the most favorable terms. But there are several small establishments for smelting in Utah Territory, most of which are at Sandy, a few miles from the Cottonwood Cañons. There are others among the Western mining districts in Bingham, Dry, and Ophir Cañons.

That which I am about to describe is conducted on

the most scientific and economical plan. It embraces
all recent improvements, by which a large waste of
mineral is prevented, and consequently it yields a good
revenue to the proprietors.

As it is not a stock-jobbing concern, and there is not
a disposition on the part of the owners to sell it, I did
not find such difficulty in obtaining information there as
I experienced on making inquiries at the Emma Mine.

On the occasion of our first visit to Salt Lake, when
Brigham Young gave us an excursion on the " Utah
Southern," although we were prevented by the rain
from a full enjoyment of the entertainment, the scientific portion of our party were highly delighted with
the inspection of the Germania Smelting and Refining
Works, eight miles from the city, where the train
stopped for an hour. We had time to go through the
buildings, which are quite extensive, and to examine
the curious processes by which the mineral is refined
from its dross and becomes pure silver. The irrepres-
sible Gail Hamilton, who always wants to see everything, and always sees everything to a good purpose,
was especially interested, as it was quite in her line.
No one can eliminate such pure shining thought from
dull matters of fact as can this gifted lady. " Now just
tell us all about it, every bit about it," she said to the
handsome young German who superintended the establishment. I thought the other ladies were more

interested in the narrator than in the processes he described.

He said that Flach, one of his countrymen, was the inventor, modestly disclaiming any merit for himself, although the company owes much to the ingenuity of his brain. It would obviously be impossible to remember all the description given by Mr. Billing, but from some notes which he kindly gave me afterwards I will endeavor to condense as much as may be of interest, without tiring the patience of general readers.

We were shown five large pots, each one capable of holding over twenty tons of base bullion. This is thrown into one of them as it is received from the various smelting works where it has been extracted from the ore. An intense heat is kept up by the furnaces until the temperature is reached at which zinc will melt.

Zinc is used for the separation of gold, silver, and copper from lead, because it has a greater affinity for these and other metals than it has for lead. When base bullion contains from one hundred and fifty to two hundred ounces of silver per ton, two or three per cent. of zinc is sufficient to separate it completely. After there is sufficient heat the zinc is gradually stirred in, and when the mass has somewhat cooled off it is found that the zinc being thoroughly mixed with the lead takes up the gold and copper with much of the silver, and rises to the surface. After a while this scum is taken off and put into another pot, when the process is renewed, and afterwards into another, renewing it again until the separation is complete ; and by means of tapping the pot the lead runs out and the pure metal remains. The whole time consumed in the operation is about twenty-four hours.

The capacity of the works is forty tons per day. The fuel used is coal and coke. The latter is now very expensive, as it is brought from Pittsburgh, Pa., at a cost of $30 per ton. When the mines of coal in Southern Utah are developed these prices will be materially reduced. The fluxes used are hematite iron ore costing $15 per ton, and lead slag which costs very little, as it is to be had on the spot. What is called the " test," by which, at the termination of all these processes, the pure silver is brought out, was by far the most interesting to us. As soon as the " cupellation" had terminated, there was what may be really styled a beautiful phenomenon of " brightening." As soon as the last trace of lead cleared itself from the silver, an instantaneous vivid flash covered the little silver sea and threw out a wonderfully pure and peculiar light. The ladies were in ecstasies over this and begged for a repetition of it, but as another twenty-four hours must have elapsed before

they could be gratified, they were forced to be contented with this one beautiful exhibition. Each of them
was presented with a bit of the silver, from which
they proposed to have made some little ornament, in
token of their appreciation of the interesting practical
lecture we had received from the courteous young
manager.

If the weather had permitted, we intended to have
not only taken a peep at Cottonwood Cañon on this
occasion, but also to have gone as far as the " Utah
Southern," for it is now completed, forty-two miles.
This road is intended to go to St. George, more than
two hundred miles further, and in the extreme south
of the Territory. As it runs through a rich agricultural
district it will doubtless prove a valuable property,
and of great importance in adding to the general
wealth. One great branch of its business will be the
transportation of coal from the San Pete mines, which
are very nearly on its track, and to which a branch
road will be constructed. These mines are really inexhaustible, and if all reports are true, as I am assured
by experts that they are, they possess the inestimable
advantage of producing coke from their coal. The
great want of all the smelting works is this kind of
fuel, which heretofore has been brought all the way
from Pennsylvania, at a cost of thirty dollars or more
per ton. Charcoal, in view of the expense of coke, is

much used for smelting purposes.   But as wood at best is scarce in Utah, and is becoming more so every day, the price of charcoal is much enhanced.   It will, therefore, be very well understood that if coke can be delivered at the works for one-quarter of the present price, an immense impetus will be given to the great mining interests of the Territory.

CHAPTER XX.

VALUABLE as are the silver mines of Utah, they form but a small part of its mineral wealth. The country abounds in coal and iron. These are tangible minerals at all times. They yield a profit to all concerned in them. The owner, the laborer, and the carrier, each with comparatively little risk, enjoys a certain gain. Mines of silver and gold are lotteries, after all, in which vastly more blanks than prizes are drawn. Many are ruined, and a few individuals made rich by speculating in them. They are like stock operations in Wall street.

Mines of coal and iron may be compared to the legitimate commerce of these United States that existed for the benefit of the whole people before ruinous legislation and a depreciated currency enriched a few, impoverished the many, and made gamblers of us all.

The southern portion of Utah, in which direction the Utah Southern and the Salt Lake Sevier Valley and Pioche Railroads, already mentioned, are rapidly extending, presents great inducements to iron manufacturers. Probably nowhere in this country can a similar extent of territory be found containing such immense deposits of iron-ore, and coal suitable in its natural condition or without coking for blast-furnace use, and limestone of the greatest purity, in juxtaposition.

The time cannot be far distant when capital will be attracted to the iron and coal mining interests. Then, instead of Utah importing railroad iron, iron castings, tools and machinery from distant parts of the country on the Atlantic and Pacific coasts, steel and iron rails will be rolled in the southern counties and all articles manufactured from iron will be furnished, not only for the requirements of the Territory, but to an extent that might supply the entire country between the two oceans.

The iron-ore is both magnetic and hematite, and remarkably rich in metallic iron, little ore being less than fifty per cent. of pure iron, while the largest proportion of all the deposits yet opened will average nearly seventy per cent.

The great complaint of iron-masters in other parts of this country and in England is, not so much of the

leanness of the ore, as of the impurities found in it.
Sulphur is often combined with the iron at a large
percentage of the whole, and phosphorus, the greatest
of all objectionable matter, is in nearly all iron-ore.

The former can be burnt out by calcining the ore
before it is used in the blast-furnace, by which process,
however, the cost of the ore is considerably enhanced ;
but phosphorus to the present time defies all attempts
to remove it entirely.   Bessemer steel, or ordinary
description of steel of good quality, cannot be made
from iron containing even less than half of one per
cent. of phosphorus.

But in Utah it is claimed the iron-ore is found, not
in veins, but in immense deposits, of such a character
that the laboratory tests show it to be free entirely from
both sulphur and phosphorus.   It is found in quantities heretofore unknown anywhere on our continent.
It may also safely be said that, excepting in Wyoming, these iron-ore and coal deposits are the only ones
of magnitude between the boundaries of Canada and
Mexico, and from the Mississippi River to the Pacific.

At present, with few exceptions, the deposits are
almost exclusively claimed and held by parties who
are too poor to go even to the expense of survey and
purchase from the United States. What is required, in
order to bring these deposits now before persons whc
are engaged in iron manufacture and mining coal, is

some little amount of capital to aid the claimants on
shares to procure the titles from the Government.
Some claimants have offered to convey half of their
claims to any one who will procure a title, and
others will do even better than this in order to attain
the same result.

By the existing laws of Congress, as understood by
the Commissioner of the Land Office, large tracts of
iron and coal lands can be procured for a small outlay
of capital. The future value of these will depend upon
their judicious selection, not as to the quantity or
quality of the iron-ore and coal, but entirely as to present and future routes of transportation, settlements,
desirability of position for furnaces and large manufacturing establishments.

It is hardly possible to go much amiss, however, in
selection of the location of iron-ore and coal deposits.
The Territory will be soon opened up in various directions by railroads, and no portion of it at an earlier
date than in the southern part.

The project of establishing blast-furnaces, puddling-
furnaces, and rolling-mills for manufacture of Bessemer steel rails, has already been agitated at Salt Lake
City. The plan proposed was to locate extensive
works in the iron country, about two hundred and
fifty miles south of Salt Lake City, for the purpose of
supplying the railroad wants of Utah and Nevada,

as well as the Southern Pacific Railroad, with iron-rails and other material.

The absolute necessity of such an establishment, the immense advantages presented in iron-ore, coal, and limestone over any other portion of the country to make it extremely profitable, has been discussed by the press and people of the Territory ; but lack of necessary capital, and of men skilled in iron manufacturing commencing from the ore-bed, have prevented the undertaking to the present time.

The coal-fields in San Pete county and Iron county have in many cases been surveyed and taken up. In the former county coal to some extent has been mined, and excellent coke made from the coal has been exhibited.

At present, however, the coke used by the smelting works near Salt Lake is brought all the way by railroad from beyond Pittsburgh, and sells, as has been stated, at thirty to thirty-five dollars per ton. At times the works are short of this kind of fuel, and occasionally have had to stop work for several days before securing a supply. Of wood and timber the whole Territory is so sparsely supplied, that coal and coke must always be the fuel for all uses.

The line of the proposed Salt Lake Sevier Valley and Pioche Railroad will open up both the iron-ore and coal deposits, by affording means of transportation at Summit Creek Cañon in Iron county, within twelve miles of the proposed road. Quite a large force of men has been at work on several locations, held by Salt Lake mining operators. Here veins of bituminous coal, from six to eight feet wide, have been opened. Specimens from the croppings down to six feet have been exhibited, and pronounced by experts very superior in quality, and free from sulphur and impurities. The geological formation at Summit Creek is sandstone and slate, similar to that in all parts of the county where coal exists; and elsewhere in the Territory where coal and iron-ore are found, the formation clearly shows them to be of the character of the coal and iron fields of Pennsylvania, Ohio, Missouri, and the Lake Superior region.

Fire-clay, and other clay, suited to building purposes and for manufacture of ware, is abundant through the Territory wherever coal and iron-ore are found. Of manganese and manganesian iron-ore there is more in quantity, and so situated as to be more cheaply mined than in any other part of the world. Speigeliesen made from the manganesian iron-ore, used in combination for smelting, and bleaching-powders from manganese, can here be manufactured in sufficient quantity to meet the wants of the entire country.

At the date of writing this work, several persons are in England with the surveys and reports on the mineral deposits of Southern Utah, endeavoring to raise capital there to open up the great interests that have been named.

Iron-ore and coal deposits, as located by discoverers, are offered for sale, or as pledges for loans to be made on them ; the money obtained is to be entirely invested in improvements and in the necessary works to develop the properties. Little success has as yet attended these efforts, for two reasons : first, in presenting the properties for sale, enormous prices have been asked ; and secondly, in proposals made for borrowing money it was seen at a glance that the parties who had the matter in hand, possessed neither the knowledge nor educated skill to manage such enterprises.

The prices asked for the properties are not near the actual values, but those who are interested in the sale should remember that one hundred dollars per acre (which has been asked) for coal and iron-ore lands situated in Southern Utah, away from not only transportation, but remote from settlements of any kind, will not be likely to attract purchasers in England. If, on the other hand, owners had offered half their land at a mere nominal price, or even given a deed of the same free of cost, on condition that it be improved, the mines opened, and furnaces and mills established, it would have made for the half held by the owners a value ten times greater than is likely to be obtained for the whole in event of sale even at prices now asked.

In fact, in all mining communities enormous prices are asked for what are but mere discoveries or prospects. As is often said, a man for a mere showing of mineral on the surface and a hole dug a few feet in the ground, and absolutely nothing more, will ask, unblushingly, a hundred or two hundred thousand dollars.

Utah, in the large prices asked heretofore for the coal and iron-ore discoveries and locations, has been particularly unfortunate. Both coal and iron-ore are articles of small market value when mined ready for use. The most extensive deposits of the greatest richness and pureness in character, away from transportation and remote from settlements, actually have no immediate value. These possess only a future value, a value when roads shall be made and people shall live along their lines.

To lead to construction of roads and to induce settlements, coal and iron properties must be presented to the public, at first, at mere nominal prices : not with the idea of obtaining purchasers at prices that will more than pay expenses incurred in locating and obtaining the government patent ; but rather to endeavor to attract buyers by low prices, and exhibits

as to what the future will give in return for the large
outlay that must be made, outside of the purchase of
the fee of the land. One or two successful coal or
iron mines operated on a large scale near the line of
roads under process of construction, would lead to
other developments, and so on, until roads would be
specially built, and people go to live near the mines.

The small iron furnaces now in operation in Utah
Territory make large returns to the owners. There is
no question but that future results will show that the
iron and coal interests of Utah far exceed in value
its mines of silver, rich as they are. The actual
"out-turn" and result in money profit, will be greater
than from all the mines and reduction works of the
precious metals.

Utah Territory, those territories adjacent, the whole
country from the Mississippi to California, will be intersected by railroads, and settled up by a numerous
and thriving population. The iron and coal to produce all this will not be brought from afar, but will be
mined and manufactured, to supply the demand, from
the deposits in Utah. There are already two small
iron furnaces in operation in the southern part of the
Territory, where coal is mined in a small way, and
though carted some distance, yet pays the parties
interested a handsome return.

Coal in San Pete county has been worked on a

moderate scale for some time, and has found its way of late to Salt Lake City. Iron-ore has been brought by the Union Pacific Railroad from some distance, to be used for flux in reduction of other ores. The cost of transportation, in both cases, interferes with or restricts the consumption. All this will be changed by and by, for the immense sources of wealth and profit pointed out as found throughout that portion of Utah, will not long remain undeveloped. The present year, I am led to believe, will not end before action will be taken directly for the working of the coal deposits, and for opening and developing the iron-ore beds.

CHAPTER XXI.

The Evanston Coal Mines.—Other Coal Mines along the Line of the Union Pacific Railroad.—Oil-bearing Rock.—Deposits of Soda and Sulphur.—Various Mineral Resources.—The Work of Oakes Ames.

ON the way home I stayed for a few hours at the Evanston coal mine, situated in the eastern part of the Territory, six miles beyond Echo Cañon.

My stay was necessarily too short to admit of a visit to the dark regions below-ground, but I fortunately met at the works Mr. T. E. Sickles, the efficient superintendent of the Union Pacific Railroad, who very kindly answered all inquiries in regard to the Evanston mines, and gave me some valuable memoranda relating to the mineral products not only in this immediate neighborhood, but all along the line of that road. As they are intimately connected with the prosperity of Utah, mention of them will not be considered out of place. Mr. Sickles says that the Evanston and other mines, scattered along by the side of the track for a distance of four hundred miles extending to Wyoming station, are inex-

haustible treasuries of bituminous coal. All these
discoveries have been made since the road was pro-
jected, and they are consequently unexpected but
welcome additions to its property value.

Coal mines have been opened at Carbon, Rock
Springs, and Evanston, and at other points on the
Union Pacific Railroad, from which were mined dur-
ing the year 1873 an aggregate of three hundred and
fifty thousand tons for the use of the Pacific and Utah
Railroads, and also for domestic consumption at all the
towns along the line of railroad between Omaha and
Sacramento.

The coal is found in strata, either horizontal or with
slight inclination, varying in thickness from a few
inches to twenty-eight feet, which latter is the thickest
vein developed up to this time. It has furnished
about one half of all the coal taken out during the
year.

The quality of the coal for domestic use, or for use
of locomotives, is known to be unsurpassed by any
bituminous coal in this country. No experiments
have been made in the manufacture of iron by the use
of this coal, and its value therefore, for this purpose,
is unknown.

Within a belt of four hundred miles long and forty
miles wide, the Union Pacific Railroad Company owns
five million one hundred and twenty thousand acres

of land, embracing a greater area of coal-fields than is contained in the entire anthracite region of Pennsylvania.

There are numerous deposits of iron-ore near the line of the railroad, extending from Cheyenne to Ogden, a distance of five hundred and sixteen miles.   Several of these ores have been analyzed, but none have been used for the manufacture of iron.   An extensive deposit of magnetic ore, which is found near Rawlins, is used in the silver-reducing furnaces in Utah as a flux.   About thirty tons a day are now shipped for that service. The ore in its natural state is ground at Rawlins and sold as a mineral paint.

For this purpose it is used on the Union Pacific Railroad for painting its cars and buildings, and has proved preferable to any other mineral paint.   During the present year a furnace will be built at Evanston, the value of the iron-ores and coal, for the manufacture of iron and Bessemer steel, having been practically determined.

On the line of the Union Pacific Railroad, near Green River, is found an inexhaustible quantity of oil-bearing rock, similar in appearance to the shale in Scotland, from which, last year, were obtained over twenty-one million gallons of lubricating and burning oil.   The Green River shale yields an average of thirty gallons of oil to the ton of rock, of which quantity fourteen gallons are lubricating oil, and six-teen gallons are of light gravity or burning oil.

Repeated tests of the rock have been made by means of a retort built for the purpose, which holds five hundred pounds of shale, and the results were singularly uniform. Ten tons of the shale have been treated in this manner, and the resultant oils have been subjected to repeated and exhaustive tests. As a lubricator, which is the chief value of the oil, it is equal to the best that has been purchased for use on the Union Pacific Railroad at a cost of thirty-three cents per gallon. The cost of producing the oils from rock does not exceed fifteen cents per gallon. During the year 1873 the Union Pacific Railroad Company paid thirty-six thousand dollars for oils used on their line for lubricating and burning. The same quality and quantity of oils can be made from the rock for fif-teen thousand dollars.

Oils made from this shale can be manufactured and sold at a handsome profit for the supply of the Pacific slope, which has hitherto obtained all its kerosene and lubricating oils from Pennsylvania, Ohio, or Virginia. During 1872 the quantity of oil sent to California from New York or Cleveland by ocean and by rail amounted to one million five hundred thousand gallons. Lubri-cating oil can also be manufactured from Green River shale, and delivered with fair profit at Pittsburgh for a less price than it now brings at the West Virginia wells.

There would therefore be a market for the lubricating oil made from shale throughout the United States. The transportation of it over the Union Pacific Railroad would add largely to its revenues, which would be still further increased by the development of the distillery works established near Green River for the manufacture of the oils.

The alkaline character of the soil for several hundred miles along the line of the Union Pacific Railroad led to the belief that deposits of soda in large quantities would eventually be discovered. Recently two soda lakes have been found about fifty miles north of the line of the railroad, which have been carefully examined and the quality of the soda determined by repeated analyses.

From one lake the water evaporated to such an extent as to leave a deposit of soda six feet in depth along its shores. This soda is entirely free from any earthy admixture. In an adjoining lake, which is much the largest, the water is a saturated solution, one-tenth of its weight being soda. The soda has a larger percentage of carbonate than the salsoda of commerce, and is therefore worth more per pound.

The report of commercial statistics of the United

States, made to Congress by the Secretary of the Treasury for 1872, states that there were imported into the United States, during that year, one hundred and eighteen thousand tons of soda, of the value of four million nine hundred and forty-five thousand seven hundred and twenty dollars, and that there were manufactured in this country soda of the value only of two hundred thirty-one thousand six hundred and forty-seven dollars, showing that ninety-five per cent. of all the soda used in this country is imported.

Soda from the line of the Union Pacific Railroad can be delivered at the Atlantic ports for ten dollars less per ton than the present selling price, while for the supply of the interior States it could be delivered for from ten to twenty dollars less per ton.

The transportation over the Union Pacific Railroad of the soda used in this country would add a very large sum annually to the earnings of the Union Pacific Railroad Company.

In Utah Territory, at a point about thirty miles south of the railroad, there was discovered last year a large deposit of sulphur.

It has been visited by several persons, who agree in the statement that the quantity is practically inexhaustible.

The discoverer of this deposit, after numerous analyses to ascertain its quality, went to Europe and

visited all the localities from which the sulphur used
in this country is obtained, to determine whether he
could successfully compete with the foreign article.
He found that the deposit in Utah is twenty per cent.
purer than any in Europe ; and, after careful investigation of all the facts, he asserts that he can deliver
sulphur at the Atlantic cities to exclude all sulphur of
importation.   If this statement be correct, the earnings from the transportation of sulphur over the railroad would be at least three hundred thousand dollars
per annum.

Such as I have enumerated are the inexhaustible
and rapidly developing mineral resources not only of
Utah, but of the approaches to it along the line of the
Union Pacific Railroad.   But a few years ago they
were not even dreamed of.   The most sanguine imaginations did not entertain the remotest idea of their
value.

The active promoter of this road, when, in the face
of every discouragement, he undertook its completion, looked chiefly at its value as a national thorough-
fare, and was totally ignorant of the mineral products
that would be found in the vicinity of almost every
station along its line.

The country will remember, if history is read aright,
that it is mainly indebted to Oakes Ames for its Union
Pacific Railroad.   He organized the Crédit Mobilier,

without which the road could not have been constructed. He undertook the enterprise when no one else dared to embark in a scheme fraught with so many dangers and uncertainties. He was a plain business man, but he was ambitious withal. His ambition was to earn the credit of accomplishing this great national work. I had it from his own lips that he would have been a richer man if he had never undertaken it.

He never dreamed of doing wrong in the distribution of the stock. The hands of Oakes Ames were never soiled by any dirty lobby transactions. His great object was to build a railroad that has united the East and the West and made our country one and indivisible. To effect this he did not hesitate to directly approach members of Congress in the most approachable way. He knew that " where the treasure was there would the heart be also."

He finished his work, and now lies beneath a simple tombstone in the churchyard of a New England village ; but the people of the great country that he has strapped together with his iron bars, may behold his monument at every point of their journey from the Atlantic to the Pacific.

OAKES AMES.

CHAPTER XXII.

IN the olden times, before railroads or even daily
mails by stage-coach were known in Utah,
"merchandizing" was a very profitable business.
The principal merchants were Gentiles, and they
made money rapidly. Only once each year could
their stocks of goods be renewed. Every spring they
would go East to buy, and every autumn their long
trains of loaded ox-wagons would reach the valley
with the new stock. There was always a great strife
among the tradesmen to be first in the market.

If a merchant failed to have his goods on the
shelves by "Conference"—the first week in Octo-
ber—he suffered severely, and was certain to be behind in his affairs the whole year. The "Fall Conference" was the great purchasing season for all
classes. Then such of the necessaries of life as the
soil of Utah failed to produce must be secured, or the

long winter must pass without them. The snow laid an embargo upon anything like free intercourse between remote sections. So at " Conference time' thousands of families flocked into the chief city, tc hear words of practical wisdom from their leaders, and to exchange their agricultural products and their savings for the contents of the stores. This was the harvest-time for the storekeepers. Their stocks were considered " fresh," for they were bought in April or May, and had been but three or four months on the journey.

The question with the tradesmen was, how to deliver the goods as fast as they were called for. Behind the counters were clerks standing close as an army file, working with might and main for twenty hours out of each twenty-four to supply the never-diminishing crowd which surged and struggled and fought good-naturedly for the foremost place. Men and women, when tired of waiting, or hopeless of reaching the counter, would wrap their money in a paper, and securing the momentary attention of some clerk, would toss the precious package over the heads of the people, to be caught by the attendant, scream out the order for tea, or sugar, or " domestics," and .catch the bundle deftly when it came.

Those were great days for the people and greater for the merchants. Prices were enormous and the profits were great. A pound of nails, costing four cents in Massachusetts, were cheap at thirty cents in Salt Lake City, as late as 1864. The freight was the principal item. Merchants in that far-off country must pay cash for their goods. It would have been folly to solicit credit from wholesale dealers in the great cities on goods designed for the heart of the wilderness and the home of the Indian.

It required capital to do business, and that capital must be idle for the months elapsing between the time of purchase and the date of sale. Money in those days would bring almost any price asked; five per cent. a month was looked upon as about fair! Of course, those who had money made money very rapidly, in whatever way they employed it. For years the great merchants were Livingston & Bell, Gilbert & Gerrish, and John Kimball, all Gentiles. Their gains were enormous. Then a young firm, composed of four brothers, the Walkers, went into trade. They were Mormons, and excellent business men. In 1862 they quietly opened a route through Utah, southward to the Pacific coast, and thence to San Francisco, and thus brought in trains of goods in the dead of winter. This enterprise gave them a great trade, and placed them far in advance of their long-established competitors.

The prominent houses soon after gave up business,

and Walker Brothers held the trade. Kimball took
in young Lawrence, a Mormon ; Jennings, also a
Mormon, who had been engaged in tanning, went
into " merchandizing," and was successful. Hooper
& Eldridge, Mormons, put their capital together and
started out in the same line. Godbe, another
"Saint," added groceries to his drug-store, and for a
time the trade was entirely in Mormon hands.

Then a co-operative store was organized at the instance of Brigham Young, and all the traders were invited to consolidate their stocks of goods in this enterprise. Walker Brothers declined, and were ultimately
cut off from the church for this and other rebellious
acts. Godbe refused, and the church cut him off also.
Jennings and the rest reluctantly fell into the co-operative ranks. Kimball, not being a Mormon, held out
till he died, and a year or two later, Lawrence, the
surviving partner, though scarcely longer affiliating
with the church, closed out the business. Walker Brothers continued in trade—extended their great stores,
added new and important features, made their establishment the most metropolitan in character and
the most attractive in appearance of any in Utah, and
to-day they divide the business of the Territory with
"Zion's Co-operative Mercantile Institution."

The last-named establishment deserves more than a
passing remark. It is the great business concern of

the West, and has not less than one hundred thousand regular customers. As a wholesale house it supplies all the Mormon stores in all parts of Utah. Its retail stores at various points do a heavy trade with saints and sinners alike. Its total receipts reach about six million dollars a year. Its paid-up capital amounts to nearly one million dollars, and new stock is always for sale at one hundred dollars per share. Its dividends average fully twenty per cent. per annum, besides a large and constantly increasing reserve.

Generally its management has been good, and its credit high. The great New York house of H. B. Claflin & Co. ships to it more than two million dollars worth of drygoods annually, and Benedict, Hall & Co. send to it every year hundreds of thousands in boots and shoes. All who supply the " Co–op," as it is laconically termed, express satisfaction with its promptness in paying its debts.

Of course, the advent of railroads has greatly changed the currents of trade in Utah. The freight on the pound of nails is no longer twenty cents, but is reduced to six cents ; and the time of its transit from the factory to its place of consumption has fallen from four months to fifteen days. As all other things lessen, so do profits. Money drops with the rest. One and a half per cent. per month is still considered a cheap rate for currency, and a large proportion of all loans bear interest at the rate of two per cent. per month, payable in advance.

The Legislature has had the good sense to enact no usury laws, which are a dead letter everywhere, and exist only to be evaded. Money earns good wages in Utah, and borrowers are able to pay large interest and still realize a profit. All kind of business is profitable. The merchants, small and great, make money, without an exception. Bankers realize splendid profits. The First National Bank of Salt Lake City, with a capital of one hundred and fifty thousand dollars, regularly announces an annual dividend of fifty per cent., besides constant additions to its reserve.

Its banking-house is as fine as anything in America, its interior being as elegant as marble, and gilding, and mirrors, and carving, and frescoes and polished wood can make it. Railroads are constructed and run at great profit. The Utah Central, extending from Ogden to Salt Lake City, is thirty-eight miles long, and cost about one million two hundred and fifty thousand dollars. Its capital stock is one million five hundred thousand dollars, and its bonded debt one million dollars. It promptly pays sixty thousand dollars a year in gold as interest on its bonded debt, and then hands over to its stockholders one hundred and eighty thousand dollars in cur-

rency, being twelve per cent. on the par value of
its stock.   At the same time it is constantly adding
to its side-tracks, its lands and buildings, and its
rolling-stock.

It is as good a railroad as any in the country of
the same length, and probably as profitable. Yet its
stock and bonds are hardly known in the East, and
can be bought in Salt Lake City when offered for
sale at about sixty-five or seventy per cent. of their
par value. This railroad enterprise shows what can
be done with capital thus employed. Its builders net
twenty per cent. per annum in cash on the investment, and their property is annually increased in value
not less than ten per cent.

The success of this enterprise finds a constant parallel in such other branches of business as are entered
upon with adequate capital. Mills for the conversion
of the native wool into cloth, of the cereals into flour,
of timber into building-material, all pay handsomely.
The mines of lead, containing silver, have proved ex-
ceptional in magnitude, although affording less precious metal to the ton than the ores of some other
mining countries. In this branch of industry fortunes
are made every year by those who have the means to
follow up intelligently the indications which crop out
upon the surface of the hills and are half-buried beneath the accumulations and upheavals of ages. As

I said before, everything pays, and I may add that money-lending pays about as well as anything to those who have money to lend.

A New York or Boston man would consider himself on the high road to ruin if he had to pay two per cent. a month for money. He could not pay that rate and compete with his neighbors who traded on their own capital. But in Utah the same man would turn the borrowed capital over, and realize for himself one or two per cent. per month after paying the high rate of interest. If a business man of large experience and extended acquaintance in Utah could borrow one million dollars in New York or any cheap money market, at ten per cent. per annum, for use in Salt Lake City and vicinity, he could lend it there on first-class security, and clear for himself ten or fifteen per cent. yearly on the whole sum.

I made the acquaintance of a Gentile who has established relations with a few capitalists in Boston, New York, San Francisco, and London. He loaned money on valuable real-estate, and on the railroad securities, at the rates of interest which I have mentioned. His transactions were large, and he assured me that he had never lost a dollar of principal or interest. The funds loaned by him belonged chiefly to Gentiles, non-residents, while the borrowers were generally Mormons. He bore the

most unqualified and earnest testimony to the
honesty, promptness, and good-faith of the Mormons as a class in all business affairs. He considered Utah the safest and best place for business on
the continent.

He admitted, however, that he found it difficult to
make capitalists comprehend the facts. When he
asked for a million dollars, they timidly sent him fifty
or a hundred thousand. With safe, thrifty applicants
for five millions, on security vastly in excess of that
amount, and as good as any in the world, he was
barely able to accommodate ten per cent. of those
who applied for loans in 1873. He predicted that a
high rate of interest would continue just as long as
every enterprise entered upon proved, as now, a source
of great profit.

With large competition, all this would change ; but
the almost boundless resources of the Territory must
be developed before competition can become effect-
ive in this direction. A thousand miles of railroad
would be demanded and would be paid for, in three or
four years from completion, out of the profits of the
traffic. The mountains of iron and coal must be
penetrated and utilized to meet the home demand.
The hills must give forth their precious deposits until
their annual product reaches a hundred millions in
silver. A multitude of enterprises await the magic

touch of capital, and would employ that capital at enormous profit in the future as in the past.

In view of all this, who shall say that money will not be worth two per cent. per month in Utah for a decade or two to come ?

CHAPTER XXIII.

IN a somewhat desultory manner I have sketched a
few of the scenes in the Mormon country over
which I have rambled. Some of the characteristics
of the people have been portrayed; not a little has
been said about their religion, and as much as was
consistent with the effort to make a small book has
been introduced to show the vast agricultural, mining,
and commercial resources of the Territory and its
neighborhood.

To the scenery no pen but that of an artist can do
adequate justice. The reader should avail himself of
that wonderful invention which performs the miracle
of removing mountains to our firesides, and after he
has welcomed them there, he should return the visit
and in the pure atmosphere not susceptible of importation by photography, behold the towering mountains
from their base and the lovely valleys from peaks
above them.

If in search of health, he should not neglect the wonderful Soda Springs where his ailments will disappear if he does not forget them before his arrival. I cannot too strongly impress upon men of weak stomachs and weak lungs the salubrity of the climate ; and, if invalids of the gentler sex can be induced to " rough it " for one summer in the wilds of Utah and of Idaho, let them be assured that they can better stand the winter's campaign. Their step in the ballroom will be more elastic, their lungs can better withstand the close air of the theatre, and the poisonous combinations of lobster-salad and ice-cream in which some of them nightly indulge will have had a partial antidote.

Some reference has been made to the route from New York to Soda Springs. This little table of distances and time may still be of service :

N. Y. to Buffalo by N. Y. Central R.R.	440	miles.
Buffalo to Chicago by Lake Shore R.R..	539	"
Chicago to Omaha by Chicago & N. W. R.R..........	490	"
Omaha to Ogden by Union Pacific R.R.	1029	"
Ogden to Salt Lake City by Utah Central R.R........................	38	"
Distance from New York to Salt Lake..	2536	"

The time occupied, if the connections are made, is four days twenty hours fifteen minutes, from New York to Ogden. If the journey is then continued to

San Francisco by the Central Pacific Railroad, there is a further distance of eight hundred and seventy-eight miles to be accomplished in two days two hours and twenty minutes. Thus the whole distance from New York to San Francisco is three thousand four hundred and fourteen miles, and the whole time occupied, six days twenty-two hours and thirty-five minutes. As the time-tables are not more exact, I cannot give the odd seconds.

The fare is, from New York to San Francisco, $139.50 currency ; New York to Ogden, $117 currency, and on the branch road from Ogden to Salt Lake City, $2.

It may be remembered that as Utah is on a line of "distinct civilization" in religion, so it is also in currency. Unfortunately paper-money is the currency of the Saints. They have a holy horror of it, too.

While they admit that it gives an enhanced value to their products, they regret that it gives it also to what they are obliged to purchase. The business men generally concede that their condition would have been greatly improved if the gold currency, which ceases to be a medium of circulation on reaching their Western border, extended throughout their Territory.

If Congress would appropriate money enough to transport all its members over the Union Pacific and Central Pacific roads to California, that they might see

how a steady currency redounds to the prosperity of
that section, the Treasury could well afford the outlay.
No appropriation is advocated for bringing them
back.

I have outlined the routes, and the time in which
the journey can be accomplished, if necessary. Most
people would prefer to loiter by the way. They can
do this with their through tickets, if they are inclined
to stop at any or all of the stations on the road.

Still, if one wishes to rush through, he need not be
deterred by a fear of fatigue. Railroad travelling is
an anomaly. You become rested by being tired.
Nine hours from New York to Boston, or Washington,
is a very irksome journey. To one who has been
obliged to take it, its frequency does not overcome
its dread.

The same sort of feeling is experienced for the first
day of a journey to the West. Afterwards you become
accustomed to it, and soon the splendid and comfortable Pullman car comes to be regarded as a home.
You feel no further fatigue during the journey.

You are obliged to keep regular hours, retiring and
rising when other people do. That is better for
you than late and uncertain hours in New York.
You are generally well entertained at the restaurants.
These are not of the best, but every year they are
improving. If you are a teetotaller, you do not need

the advice which is worthy the attention of those who, if they are of opposite principles, may thank me for it.

It is, to be provided with your own wine and spirits. Everything of this kind on the road is abominable— more so even than the sloppy tea and weak imitations of coffee at the temperance restaurants.

You cannot fail to make pleasant acquaintances in your constantly moving house. The practice of whist and euchre will make you perfect in these games. But never dare to play with a stranger in the filthy smoking-car. Beware of the "Three Card Monte" man! You will be all the better for ignorance of this pretty little amusement.

Yes, indeed, you may pass away your time most agreeably on the road; for, of course, you will have a portable library, and the guide-books will occupy much of your mental digestion.

The rate of speed not being very great, reading is easy, especially on the Union Pacific, where the line runs for hundreds of miles over a level prairie, and, whether owing to this cause or to its solid construction I know not, it is one of the smoothest roads that I ever travelled upon in any part of the world.

Thus much for the railroad journey. But when once in Utah or in any part of the West that you have time to explore, go where the railroad has not yet penetrated. Alas for the lover of nature, he will find that iron monster chasing him everywhere ! Its march is onward, over and under mountains, crossing mighty rivers, winding through the loveliest valleys, the mad devil on its track waking the dreamy solitudes of the wilderness from the repose of ages into the activity of business life.

Then, before this terrible railroad is omnipresent— before saddles and even walking-boots become things of the past—ride and tramp ! for that is the way to see that best part of the world which nature still claims for her own.

CHAPTER XXIV.

IN my wanderings among the Mormon people I may have been too much attracted by the poetry of their primitive and pastoral life, and too grateful for their hospitality, to criticise them severely.

Why should I? I don't believe in their revelations; and God forbid that I should be understood as attempting to justify polygamy. Mormonism is not my religion, nor polygamy my practice. But for all that, if I knew that the press, supposing it to notice this little book, would abuse me unmercifully, and if the "forty-thousand parson-power" of all the pulpits should come down with its anathemas, I will say this: in all my voyages and travels about the world, I never before passed three months in a community more industrious, upright, honest in dealing among themselves and with others, quiet, inoffensive, loyal to government, temperate, virtuous, and religious, than these Mormons.

With all its impositions and absurdities, a religion that will produce results like these must have in it of good,—something. Yes, a great deal!

Lest injustice should be done to the Gentile population of the Territory, let me explain, if I have not already done so by implication, that this small outside element does not fairly represent Eastern civilization.

Most of the non-Mormons whom I have styled Gentiles in accordance with the general acceptation of the term, are those who come for temporary purposes of trading, mining, and other speculations. The greater part of them are without families, and frequently they are from the lowest walks of life.

In his tales of Mining Camps, Bret Harte has aptly described this class. He can scarcely be said to have exaggerated. I found there just such men.

In the City of Salt Lake the Gentile population is different. There are two classes of them. One is of ladies and gentlemen fitted to adorn society anywhere, families who chiefly from considerations of permanent business take up their residence in the Territory. There is another set of Gentiles in the same town who would like to introduce gambling-houses, drinking-saloons, and brothels, to civilize the Mormons.

The respectable people first mentioned rarely have any difficulty with the dominant sect. Although they are more or less exclusive, they frequently meet the Mormon ladies and gentlemen in society—as do likewise the officers of Camp Douglas and their wives.

It may be said with truth that if the Gentile inhabitants of Utah were all such as these, there would be scarcely a word of complaint against the Mormons, and no petitions to Congress for relief from the tyranny of the Church.

These petitions come mostly from recusant disciples, people of no especial standing in the community, and small politicians.

That some very worthy men are induced to sign them is undoubtedly true, but the proportion is very small. Every year the petitions accumulate at Washington, and serve the turn of some virtuous statesman in framing a bill of extermination.

At present, another strong effort is being made to induce Congress to legislate so that the individual interests of these malcontents may be benefited. Their shafts are generally aimed at the target of polygamy, about which most of the petitioners do not care a straw.

A great many of them would like to see real-estate and other securities depressed. There are " bears " in Salt Lake as well as in Wall street. There are politicians there as well as in Washington. These would like to wrest political power from the Mormons to appropriate it to themselves.

At my request Hon. Geo. Q. Cannon, the Utah delegate to Congress, has forwarded me their last memorial, with a counter-memorial from the legislature.

The first commences as follows:

NON-MORMON CITIZENS OF UTAH.

" Memorial of a Committee of forty-five gentlemen, selected at a Public meeting of non-Mormon residents and voters of Salt Lake City, in the Territory of Utah, held on the 19th of January, 1874, to prepare a memorial to Congress, setting forth the grievances of the non-Mormon people of said Territory, and for such legislation by Congress as is needed for the full protection of all classes of people residing in said Territory. February 9, 1874.—Referred to the Committee on the Territories and ordered to be printed.

" *To the Senate and House of Representatives in Congress assembled :*—We, the undersigned committee, selected at a public meeting of the non-Mormon voters of Salt Lake City, held on the 19th of January, 1874, in pursuance of the following resolution passed at said meeting, to wit—

" *Resolved,* That the committee of forty-five appointed by this meeting are hereby instructed to prepare, at their earliest convenience, a memorial to Congress, setting forth the grievances of the non-Mormons of Utah, and requesting such legislation by Congress as is needed for the full protection of all classes of people residing in this Territory—

" Respectfully represent :

" That the political status of the Territory of Utah is anomalous in this, that five-sixths or more of the entire population are members of an organization, the adherents of which claim that it is religious in its character, while in fact it enjoins, both as to faith and practice, the commission of the highest crimes.

"Polygamy is openly and defiantly practised in the face of the law of Congress, and the doctrine of the shedding of blood for the remission of sins has been preached from the Mormon pulpit, and deliberately published in the official organs of the church. See the following discourse of Brigham Young, delivered in the Tabernacle and published in the "Journal of Discourses," vol. i., p. 82, which book is in the Public Library at the Capitol."

It is chiefly filled with quotations from Brigham Young's sermons on "blood atonement," none of them of a later date than 1856, since which time it is well known that the doctrine has not been publicly advocated.

It closes in this way :

"Thus, by an abuse and perversion of the powers granted in the organic act, a theocracy most despotic in its character has been kept in actual operation for twenty years, and will continue for many more, unless Congress shall sooner enact such laws as will place it beyond the power of the Mormon Church to call to its aid the forms of law in the administration of its government.

"As long as Brigham Young, as the head of the church, is permitted to retain his power, to execute or defeat the execution of the laws according to his will, his misguided and credulous adherents will continue to implicitly obey and believe him, and that his mission is divine and his authority paramount to and beyond the reach of human laws. But, once take away from him the form of law under which he has so cunningly acquired and exercised theocratic rule, and then the mission of the Mormon Church, as a governing power in municipal affairs, will, as it should, soon come to an end.

" Therefore, the affairs of this Territory being ano-malous, we respectfully submit that special legislation is right and proper, and ask your honorable body to pass at an early day such legislation as will remedy the existing evils ; and we give it as our opinion that the bills introduced by Senators Logan and Freling-huysen would either of them effectually accomplish that end."—JOSEPH R. WALKER AND OTHERS.

The counter-memorial is as follows :

MEMORIAL OF THE LEGISLATIVE ASSEMBLY OF UTAH,

Asking for a commission of investigation to be sent to Utah to inquire into all alleged abuses in affairs there.   February 16, 1874.—Referred to the Com-mittee on the Judiciary and ordered to be printed.

To the honorable the Senate and House of Re-presentatives of the United States in Congress as-sembled.—GENTLEMEN : We, your memorialists, the legislative assembly of the Territory of Utah, respect-fully represent that whereas a large majority of the people of this Territory are accused of disloyalty, insubordination, and other violations of the Constitu-tion and laws of the United States ; and whereas these accusations are absolutely untrue, and are made with malicious intent to procure proscriptive legisla-tion by Congress : Therefore, being anxious that legislation, if upon thorough investigation any should be deemed necessary, should be such as will con-duce to the greatest good of all, we respectfully and earnestly solicit your honorable body to send to Utah a commission of investigation, with instructions to inquire into all alleged abuses in our territorial affairs, and with authority to send for persons and papers

needed in the prosecution of their inquiries. And we further respectfully ask your honorable body, for the protection of what we deem the best interests of the whole people of the Territory, to suspend all action, so far as special legislation for Utah is concerned, until such time as said commission shall have had opportunity to investigate and report; and for a course so conducive to wise and consequently beneficial legislative action, we, your memorialists, will ever pray.   LORENZO SNOW,
President of the Council,
and the other members of the Legislature.

With the documents I received the following note:

DEAR SIR : I send you herewith the memorials sent down from Utah, also an argument by Hon. Thos. Fitch made last year. From these you may get some ideas and save me from dwelling at length on the features of the recent memorial. You will perceive that they (the memorialists) complain of the murders which have been committed and the murderers unpunished, and yet they say the Courts have had full power to try such cases, but have not exerted it. If there are murderers at large the Mormons are not to blame. The Probate Courts have punished crime whenever evidence has warranted, whether its perpetrators have been Mormons or non-Mormons.

In many instances, as if to thwart the Probate Courts, the Judges of District Courts, particularly Judge McKean, have released criminals on writs of *habeas corpus.* As far as the murder of Dr. Robinson is concerned, every effort has been made to fasten that upon the Mormons, a man going so far as to perjure himself (as he afterwards swore) to implicate certain reputable citizens of Salt Lake City. This man's name was Baker. But though ex-Gov. Weller, of

Cal., spent a considerable time after that murder in investigating it, no clue could be obtained that led to the implication of any Mormon ; and it was charged, at that time, in the public prints of Salt Lake City, that when Weller found that the investigation was likely to lead away from the Mormons and to fasten the crime elsewhere, he closed it.

As for the Mountain Meadows affair, ex-Gov. Young did proffer to go with the Judges to the South and promote by his influence the full investigation of that slaughter. It would have been too good an evidence in favor of Mormon disposition to do right to be accepted, and would have spoiled an excellent tale of Mormon atrocities. So it has stood. But I need not go through with all these charges. I am confident that in no Territory of the United States have there been so few murders unpunished, or where life and property have been so safe, as in Utah. That the people are patient and forbearing, is evidenced by the fact that such men as those who have for years persistently and malignantly slandered them, are permitted to walk undisturbed in the Territory.

While I may not agree with many of your views and deductions, I think your book, as the result of personal observation, in so far as I understand its spirit, cannot fail to do good. Differences of opinion, honestly entertained and frankly stated, should always be tolerated and respected. No one ought to fear them.

With kind regards, I am,

Respectfully,

GEO. Q. CANNON.

Whatever grounds the non-Mormons may have for complaint, it cannot but seem reasonable to any unprejudiced mind that the investigation asked for by the Legislature, should be had before any decided steps are taken by Congress, especially if the Constitution has to be invaded to meet the supposed exigency of the case.

If, as the non-Mormons say, a majority of six to one make oppressive laws to operate against the small minority, it would seem still more unjust if Congress should put a law-making and law-enforcing power into the hands of this small minority, to be exercised against the great majority !

I have heard the majority computed to be much larger than these gentlemen estimate it. It is supposed to be nine to one. They probably refer to the population of Salt Lake City.

It would come to this : that one-tenth of the population of the Territory, and that by no means the most reputable, composed of men who have for the most part taken up a temporary residence there, are to hold in subjection the lives and property of the other nine-tenths of the men whose fathers and many of themselves took possession of this waste land when it was Mexican territory, and with hardship, toil, and privation reclaimed it from a desert waste, developed its resources, and made it such a rich addition to the Union.

We should not attempt to excuse ourselves for this gross injustice by the plea that courts and juries of Mormons do not punish for polygamy, a crime we hold in abhorrence. While our courts at home do punish bigamists, let us acknowledge that they do not adequately deal with gambling, drunkenness, and prostitution; crimes which the Mormons hold in abhorrence, for they never fail to take cognizance of them.

Remembering that we are not immaculate ourselves, reflecting that if we were to undertake summarily to punish criminal immorality at home, we should stir up riot and murder in our streets—let us consider well before taking violent and unconstitutional measures against the Mormons which would surely antagonize a people now thoroughly loyal to Government, would check enterprise, reduce the value of property, and in no sense whatever could be productive of good.

By the treaty with Mexico, when the Territory embracing Utah was ceded to this country, it was stipulated that as soon as a portion of it contained the requisite number of inhabitants, States should be formed and admitted to the Union.

This compact has been carried out with other communities of much smaller populations than Utah possesses. We are keeping her out in the cold until polygamy is discarded, notwithstanding her persistent knocking at our doors. That is punishment enough. Utah cannot stand there long with this heavy burden on her shoulders, while all her neighboring sisters are welcomed into our family.   The religion of these Latter-Day Saints is a very heavenly one in theory, but a very worldly one in practice.   They well know the advantages of State organization.   Their desire to obtain it will speedily cause them to abandon their cherished institution.   This inducement, united with other influences already mentioned, will give a death-blow to polygamy, without the intervention of .Congress. Caustic is not the remedy for this sore.

In closing, I may venture to express the hope that some little instruction as well as amusement may have been derived from a perusal of these pages.   My Mormon friends will say that their kindness is ill-requited by adverse criticism of their doctrines and practices.   My Gentile readers will say that I have been so fascinated with the country and the people of Utah that I have given them unmerited praise.   Both verdicts will be gratefully accepted as proofs of the impartiality claimed for the book.

FINIS.